Mantras of Love
Based on Hindu Wisdom
40-Day
Marriage
Transformation
AJIT KUMAR
Relationship Coach, Mediator
& Family Lawyer

Mantras of Love

40 Day Marriage Transformation

(Based on Hindu Wisdom)

A Soul Searching Journey to Strengthen Marriage by a Relationship Coach

AJIT KUMAR

Relationship Coach, Certified Mediator and Family Lawyer

LEGAL MIND

Books-New Delhi

To Contact Ajit Kumar for speaking arrangements and coaching, please email legalmindajitkumar@gmail.com

SELF-HELP/INSPIRATIONAL

Published in India by Legal Mind.

ISBN : 978-81-924969-2-4
₹ 385/-/$ 4.5 (e-book)
$ 13.9 (paperback)

Table of Content

Description

Mantras of Love: 40-Day Marriage Transformation
A Journey to Strengthen and Deepen Your Marriage

Rekindle Love. Foster Connection. Cultivate Trust.

Marriage is a profound union—one that requires care, commitment, and continuous growth. While love is the foundation, every relationship encounters challenges such as misunderstandings, emotional distance, or misalignment of values. Whether you are newlyweds or have been together for decades, maintaining a strong marriage takes intentional effort. But where can we find the wisdom to build a relationship that thrives?

This book draws inspiration from ancient teachings, offering practical insights to help couples nurture love, strengthen communication, and foster a deep emotional connection. Rooted in time-honored wisdom, these lessons provide valuable guidance to restore harmony and cultivate a fulfilling partnership.

40-Day Journey to a Stronger Relationship

Mantras of Love: 40-Day Marriage Transformation is a structured guide designed to help you and your partner reconnect and create a lasting bond. Over 40 days, this book will lead you through key principles essential for a successful marriage, encouraging reflection and meaningful action.

Each day includes:

Core Principle – A powerful idea to enrich your relationship.
Insightful Reflection – A thought-provoking lesson to inspire growth.

Practical Step – Actionable ways to integrate these lessons into daily life.

Following this guided journey, you will learn how to:

- Build trust and strengthen communication.
- Revitalize emotional and physical intimacy.

- Resolve conflicts with understanding and patience.
- Develop deeper empathy and appreciation for your partner.
- Align your relationship with values that foster long-term happiness.

A Fresh Perspective on Love and Commitment

Unlike traditional relationship books, **Mantras of Love** blends ancient wisdom from **Hindu Scriptures- the Bhagavad Gita, Ramayana, Mahabharta and Vedas** with modern relationship dynamics, offering a holistic approach to marital fulfillment. This book encourages self-reflection, accountability, and a commitment to shared growth.

It is not about fixing your partner but about **deepening your own understanding** of love, partnership, and emotional well-being. By taking this journey together, couples can create a space where love flourishes naturally.

Who Is This Book For?

- Couples who want to **enhance their connection** and strengthen their love.
- Those experiencing **challenges in their marriage** and seeking solutions.
- Individuals looking to incorporate **spiritual wisdom** into their relationships.
- Anyone committed to fostering a **relationship based on trust, respect, and devotion**.

Whether you are working through difficulties or simply want to nurture a deeper connection, this book offers the tools to create a lasting, loving partnership.

Time-Honored Wisdom for Modern Relationships

The teachings found in this book emphasize essential relationship values such as:

The significance of **commitment and shared purpose** in a thriving marriage.

The importance of **selflessness and understanding** in fostering harmony.

How **resilience and emotional strength** can deepen your bond.

Strategies for **effective communication and conflict resolution**.

The power of **forgiveness and moving forward together**.

By applying these timeless insights, you will discover new ways to experience love, connection, and mutual support.

A Journey of Love, Healing, and Growth

Marriage is not about avoiding difficulties but about growing through them together. Love is a choice that must be nurtured every day. When both partners are committed to learning and evolving, their relationship becomes stronger and more resilient.

If you are ready to:

- **Deepen trust and strengthen your bond**,
- **Reignite passion and appreciation**,
- **Create a lasting, fulfilling relationship**,
- **Develop a meaningful, spiritual connection**,

Then this book is for you.

Your Journey Starts Now

Are you ready to embark on a path of transformation and renewed love?

Day 1 awaits. Let's begin.

WEEK 1: FOUNDATION OF LOVE (KINDNESS & PATIENCE)

Day 1: No Negativity –Avoid Criticism or Harsh Words

Day 2: Acts of Kindness – A Small Gesture of Love

Day 3: Listen With Love – Give Full Attention

Day 4: Appreciation Letter – Celebrate Their Strengths

Day 5: Small Gift of Love – A Surprise Gesture

Day 6: Quality Time – Prioritize Each Other

Day 7: Pray for Your Marriage – Seek Divine Blessings

DAY 1: NO NEGATIVITY –AVOID CRITICISM OR HARSH WORDS

Either don't give any reaction today or use pleasant words only.

Sanskrit Wisdom: "Satyam bruyat priyam bruyat na bruyat satyam apriyam."
(Speak the truth in a pleasant way, but never speak an unpleasant truth.)
— Manusmriti 4.138

Words have the power to uplift or wound. In Indian families, elders advice speaking in a manner that soothes the heart. Recall how Lord Rama, even during exile, maintained dignity in his speech.

Today on the first day, if your spouse tries to press your trigger points or instigate with harsh words. Remember, you don't have to react, try either to keep mum or speak in a pleasant way. Use only loving or uplifting words.
Example: If your spouse forgets something important, avoid saying, "You never remember anything!" Instead, say, "I know you have a lot on your mind; let's find a way to keep track together."
Ancient Wisdom:

"Speak the truth in a way that uplifts, and avoid words that hurt, even if they are true."

Words shape relationships. They can be a source of comfort or create lasting wounds. In many Indian homes, elders emphasize *"madhur vachan"*—gentle and pleasant speech—as the foundation of a peaceful household.

Imagine a young couple in a traditional Indian family. The wife forgets to prepare tea for her husband one morning. Instead of reacting harshly, the husband smiles and says, *"No worries, today is my turn to surprise you with chai!"* His warmth transforms a moment of forgetfulness into an act of care.

This principle holds true for great leaders in Indian history as well. **Lord Rama**, despite facing exile and betrayal, maintained dignity in his words. Even when speaking to those who wronged him, he upheld respect. Contrast this with rulers who spoke with arrogance—often leading to their downfall.
The lesson? Harsh words, even when truthful, can create distance. Love, when expressed with patience, nurtures deeper understanding.

Example:
Your spouse forgets something important—an errand, a call, or a special date. Instead of reacting with frustration:
"You always forget things! Why do I have to remind you every time?"
Try this instead:

"I know you have a lot on your plate. How about we set reminders together so we don't miss important things?"

A simple shift in tone and intent can turn a moment of tension into teamwork.

An Anecdote from Indian Culture:

In a small village in Gujarat, an elderly couple had been married for 50 years. Their secret? The husband never spoke harshly to his wife, even when annoyed. Once, when she burnt the rotis, instead of complaining, he smiled and said, *"Crispy ones remind me of my childhood!"* His kindness made their bond stronger. Over the years, this habit of gentle speech became their greatest strength.

Practical Ways to Speak with Love:

1. **Pause Before Reacting:** Take a deep breath before

responding in anger.

2. **Rephrase Criticism as a Suggestion:** Instead of *"You never listen,"* try *"I feel happiest when I know you're really hearing me."*
3. **Choose the Right Moment:** Avoid serious discussions when either of you is upset. A calm mind leads to better conversations.
4. **Practice the "Golden Rule":** Speak to your spouse the way you'd like to be spoken to.
5. **End the Day with Kind Words:** No matter how the day went, say one loving thing before sleeping.

A marriage built on kind words stands strong even in difficult times. Love, when expressed through warmth and patience, turns a house into a home.

DAY 2: ACTS OF KINDNESS – A SMALL GESTURE OF LOVE

Do one unexpected act of kindness.

Ancient Wisdom:

"Paropakarartham idam shareeram."

"Our body is meant for serving others." – (Bhagavata Purana 10.22.35)

Love flourishes in the little things—the small, thoughtful acts that show we genuinely care. In Indian traditions, kindness (*karuna*) is deeply rooted in relationships, often considered an expression of devotion. Whether in family life, friendships, or marriage, true love is not measured by material gifts but by selfless service.

A timeless example is found in the **Ramayana**. During their exile, **Sita would gather food and prepare meals for Rama and Lakshmana**, ensuring they remained nourished even in the harshest conditions. To her, these acts were not obligations but natural expressions of love. Likewise, Lakshmana's unwavering dedication to his brother and sister-in-law—standing guard through sleepless nights—showed how kindness strengthens bonds.

This principle applies to modern relationships, too. A simple gesture, like making tea for your spouse or handling a task they usually do, can speak volumes. These thoughtful actions create an unspoken language of love that keeps a marriage strong.

Example:

Imagine your spouse has had a long and exhausting day. They return home, visibly drained. Instead of waiting for them to ask

for help, step in with an unexpected act of kindness:
Prepare their favorite snack or beverage as a comforting surprise.
Take over a daily chore—whether it's washing dishes, folding clothes, or organizing their workspace.
Offer a moment of peace—turn off distractions, dim the lights, and create a relaxing space just for them.
These seemingly small gestures build emotional warmth and strengthen the bond between partners.

A Story from Indian Life:

In a small village in Rajasthan, an elderly couple, Mohan and Radha, had a simple morning ritual. Every day before sunrise, Mohan would wake up early and warm water for Radha's bath, without fail. He never spoke about it; it was simply his way of caring for her. Years later, when Mohan fell ill, Radha silently took over the same ritual, ensuring he had everything he needed before he even asked.

When a neighbor once asked Radha why she continued this small act, she smiled and said, *"Love isn't about grand gestures. It's about knowing what the other person needs before they say a word."*
Their story reminds us that true affection is woven into daily life—not in big, dramatic ways, but in quiet, consistent acts of kindness.

How to Incorporate Kindness in Daily Life:

1. **Prepare a Comforting Surprise** – If your spouse loves tea or coffee, make them a cup before they even ask.
2. **Take Over a Routine Chore** – If they usually do the laundry or cook, surprise them by handling it instead.
3. **Give Undivided Attention** – Put away your phone and listen to them wholeheartedly.
4. **Offer Unexpected Encouragement** – Leave a small note of

appreciation where they'll find it.

5. **Allow Them to Rest** – If they had a tiring day, encourage them to take a nap while you manage household tasks.

In marriage, **small acts of kindness add up to a lifetime of love**. By being mindful and proactive in showing care, we create a relationship filled with warmth, understanding, and appreciation.

DAY 3: LISTEN WITH LOVE – GIVE FULL ATTENTION

Listen With Love – Genuinely listen to your spouse.

Ancient Wisdom:

"Shrutam cha kritam cha bahu darshitam cha."
"True wisdom begins with listening." – (Mahabharata)

Listening is not merely about hearing words; it is about understanding emotions, validating feelings, and making your spouse feel valued. In Indian traditions, deep listening is considered a sacred practice—whether it is disciples listening to their gurus or family members absorbing life lessons from elders. The way we listen determines the strength of our relationships.

Think of the bond between **Krishna and Draupadi**. Throughout her trials, Krishna was her unwavering support, not just because he offered help, but because he truly **listened**. He never dismissed her concerns or interrupted with premature solutions—he first gave her space to express herself fully. It was this deep emotional connection that made Draupadi trust Krishna above all.

Similarly, in a marriage, when a spouse speaks, they are not always looking for immediate answers. Sometimes, they simply need to feel heard. When we listen **with patience, empathy, and without distractions**, we create an environment where love and trust can flourish.

Example:

Imagine your spouse is venting about a frustrating situation at work. You have two choices:

Half-hearted Listening: You nod absentmindedly while scrolling through your phone, occasionally saying, *"Hmm... yeah, that's tough."*

Wholehearted Listening: You put your phone down, make eye

contact, and say, *"That sounds stressful. Do you want to talk more about it?"*
The second response makes them feel truly valued, reinforcing emotional security in the relationship.

A Story from Everyday Life:

In a busy Mumbai household, Amit and Neha had been married for five years. Their days were packed with work, family responsibilities, and social obligations. Amit often found himself exhausted by the time Neha wanted to share her thoughts about the day. His usual response? A distracted *"That's nice"* or *"Oh, really?"* while scrolling through messages.

One evening, Neha decided to stop mid-sentence. Amit, still glued to his phone, didn't even notice. Frustrated, she said, *"If you won't listen, what's the point of me sharing?"*

That night, Amit reflected on their early days—how they once spoke for hours, truly engaging with each other. He decided to change. The next day, when Neha began speaking, he set aside his phone, turned towards her, and listened attentively. To his surprise, she smiled, spoke more openly, and they ended up laughing together—something they hadn't done in a while.
That simple shift—**choosing to be fully present**—revived the warmth in their relationship.

Ways to Practice Active Listening in Your Marriage:

1. **Eliminate Distractions** – Keep your phone aside and focus entirely on your spouse.
2. **Make Eye Contact** – It shows that you value what they are saying.
3. **Don't Interrupt** – Let them finish speaking before responding.
4. **Validate Their Feelings** – Instead of offering

immediate solutions, say things like *"That sounds frustrating"* or *"I understand why you feel this way."*

5. **Use Small Encouragements** – A reassuring nod, a smile, or a simple *"Tell me more"* can make a big difference.

Listening is a **silent act of love**, but its impact is profound. In a world filled with noise and distractions, the gift of your full attention is one of the most powerful ways to express care, respect, and love for your spouse.

DAY 4: APPRECIATION LETTER – CELEBRATE THEIR STRENGTHS

Write 10 things you love about your spouse.

Timeless Wisdom:

"Maitreem bhajata akhila hrith jethreem."
"Foster friendship, for it wins over every heart." – Vedic Hymn

---

A strong marriage is built on **recognition and gratitude.** In Indian culture, relationships flourish when partners express appreciation rather than take each other for granted. **Love is not just about grand romantic gestures; it is found in daily acts of kindness and recognition.**

Consider the way **Krishna honored the devotion of those around him**—whether it was Radha's unwavering love, Sudama's humility, or Arjuna's courage. He never let a kind act go unnoticed. A marriage thrives on the same principle: **making your spouse feel valued and cherished.**

In many homes, we express gratitude for food before eating, for teachers before learning, and for elders before receiving blessings. But how often do we pause to appreciate our life partners? **Small words of gratitude can transform the emotional atmosphere of a relationship.**

Example:

Imagine your spouse has had a long, tiring day. As they finally settle down, they find a handwritten note tucked into their book:

"I see how much effort you put into making our lives better. You inspire me every day."
"Your patience and kindness make our home a happier place."

"Thank you for always standing by my side. I am lucky to share this life with you."

A few thoughtful words can lift the weight of exhaustion and replace it with warmth and reassurance.

A Story from Everyday Life:
After eight years of marriage, **Amit and Priya** found themselves caught in the daily grind—work, home, responsibilities. Though they loved each other, appreciation had become **silent, assumed rather than spoken.**

One evening, Priya found an envelope with her name on it. Inside was a heartfelt letter from Amit, listing ten things he loved about her—her laughter, her resilience, her ability to make every festival special. Tears welled in her eyes as she realized **how much those words meant**. From that day, she made it a habit to leave him small notes of gratitude, reigniting the warmth in their relationship.

Simple Ways to Show Appreciation:

1. **Write a Letter:** List ten things you love about your spouse and leave it where they will find it.
2. **Sticky Notes Surprise:** Hide little notes in unexpected places—on the fridge, inside their wallet, or on their car dashboard.
3. **Random Appreciation Text:** Send a message in the middle of the day just to say, *"I appreciate you."*
4. **Public Acknowledgment:** Compliment your spouse in front of family or friends.
5. **Daily Words of Affirmation:** Start the morning with a kind statement like, *"I am grateful for you."*

Appreciation does not need a special occasion. When love is nurtured with gratitude, it grows stronger every day.

DAY 5: SMALL GIFT OF LOVE – A SURPRISE GESTURE

Give a heartfelt surprise to your spouse.

Ancient Wisdom:

"Yajna dana tapaḥ karma na tyajyam."

"Acts of giving and selfless service should never be abandoned." – Bhagavad Gita 18.5

Love flourishes in the little things we do for each other. A **thoughtful surprise, no matter how small, can create moments of joy and deepen connection**. In Indian culture, offering gifts is a long-standing tradition, often seen as a **symbol of love, gratitude, and devotion**—whether it's offering sweets to the divine, feeding a guest, or gifting a loved one on a special occasion.

The essence of a meaningful gift is not in its price but in the **emotion behind it**. A loving gesture—like making a cup of tea without being asked or leaving a heartfelt note—can brighten your spouse's day.

A well-known example of meaningful giving is Lord Krishna's unwavering support for Draupadi. When she faced humiliation in the Kaurava court, Krishna extended her sari infinitely, shielding her dignity. This was not a material gift but an **act of love, protection, and care**—the highest form of giving.

In the same way, **a small, sincere gesture can make your spouse feel seen, valued, and loved.**

Example:

Suppose your partner comes home feeling drained after a long day. Instead of diving into routine conversations, you greet them

with their favorite homemade snack and a note that says:
"You work so hard every day. I just wanted to do something small to make you smile."
This simple, unexpected act can **lift their mood and re inforce your emotional bond.**

A Real-Life Story:
Amit and Priya had been married for over a decade. While they loved each other, the routine of daily life had left little room for surprises. One morning, as Priya rushed to get ready for work, she found a small packet next to her bag. Inside was a tiny keychain with her name engraved on it and a note from Amit:
"Just a little reminder that no matter how busy life gets, you are always on my mind."
Priya smiled the whole way to work. The gift itself was small, but the **thoughtfulness behind it spoke volumes.**

Simple Ways to Surprise Your Spouse:

1. **Bring Their Favorite Snack or Dessert:** A small treat shows that you remember what they love.
2. **Write a Love Note:** Slip a short, affectionate message into their bag, wallet, or under their pillow.
3. **Give a Symbolic Gift:** Something meaningful—like a book they once mentioned, a flower from your garden, or a playlist of songs you both love.
4. **Offer an Act of Service:** Take over a small responsibility they usually handle, like making morning tea, setting up their workspace, or organizing their things.
5. **Recreate a Special Moment:** Plan a surprise that reminds them of a special time in your relationship, like cooking a meal you had on your first date.

Love is not just in big gestures but in **small, thoughtful actions** that remind your spouse they are deeply cherished. A surprise gift doesn't need to be grand—**it only needs to come from the heart.**

DAY 6: QUALITY TIME – PRIORITIZE EACH OTHER

Spend 30 minutes doing what your spouse enjoys.

Ancient Wisdom:

"Sangacchadhwam samvadadhwam."

"Walk together, speak together in harmony." – Rig Veda 10.191.2

With the demands of modern life, couples often struggle to find time for each other. Work, responsibilities, and digital distractions can create distance, even in the closest relationships. However, love isn't just about grand declarations—it's about **consistently choosing to be present** for your spouse.

Indian culture has long emphasized the significance of shared time in marriage. Whether it's **having morning tea together, going for evening strolls, or engaging in spiritual discussions**, small acts of togetherness help nurture a relationship. **Radha and Krishna's companionship is a timeless example**—they found joy in simple moments, whether it was playing by the riverbanks or having heartfelt conversations in Vrindavan. Their love wasn't about extravagant gestures, but about the **depth of their connection**.

Quality time isn't just about being physically together; it's about **being mentally and emotionally present**. It means listening, engaging, and creating moments that strengthen your bond.

Example:

If your spouse enjoys reading, **ask about their favorite book or listen to them share an interesting passage**. If they love music, **play their favorite song while you cook together**. These simple acts show that you value their interests and enjoy their company.

Likewise, if your spouse likes to unwind with a cup of tea in the evening, **sit beside them, share your day, and simply be present in the moment**. Even **a short, meaningful conversation can be more valuable than hours spent in the same space without interaction**.

A Real-Life Story:

Aditi and Rohan, a married couple with two young children, barely had time to talk beyond daily routines. One evening, Rohan noticed that Aditi had started watering the plants every night after the kids slept. Instead of scrolling through his phone, he decided to join her. **They would water the plants together, talk about their day, and laugh over little things.** What started as a small act became a daily ritual that strengthened their connection without requiring extra time in their packed schedules.

Moral: It's not about making time—it's about using everyday moments to connect meaningfully.

Ways to Prioritize Quality Time:

1. **Start or End the Day Together** – Have morning tea, pray together, or take a short walk before bed.
2. **Tech-Free Moments** – Dedicate at least 30 minutes without screens to focus on each other.
3. **Rediscover Old Traditions** – Bring back small rituals from your early days, like playing a game or cooking together.
4. **Engage in a Shared Activity** – Whether it's gardening, music, yoga, or simply reminiscing, doing things together fosters closeness.
5. **Celebrate Small Wins Together** – Acknowledge each other's achievements, no matter how small, and make time to appreciate them.

Final Thought:

Spending time together **doesn't require elaborate planning—**

it simply requires **attention and intention**. In many Indian marriages, companionship is considered a sacred bond that grows stronger when nurtured with love and care.

Your Challenge: Find one everyday moment to connect with your spouse today—whether through a shared activity, a heartfelt conversation, or simply sitting together in comfortable silence.

DAY 7: PRAY FOR YOUR MARRIAGE – SEEK DIVINE BLESSINGS

Seek divine blessings from God for your marriage.

Sacred Wisdom:

"Dharmo rakshati rakshitah."

"Those who uphold righteousness are protected by it." – Manusmriti 8.15

Marriage is more than just a partnership; it is a sacred commitment, a promise to support and uplift each other through life's journey. In Indian culture, prayers and rituals have long been considered essential for strengthening relationships and inviting harmony into married life.

Throughout history, couples have sought divine blessings to nurture their bond. One of the most revered examples is **Lord Rama and Sita**, whose relationship was built on mutual respect, unwavering commitment, and adherence to righteousness (*dharma*). Despite enduring challenges, their faith in each other and the divine helped them remain steadfast in their love.

In modern times, spirituality in marriage does not necessarily mean elaborate rituals. It can be as simple as **expressing gratitude, offering a small prayer together, or setting an intention for harmony and understanding.** This shared practice can create a deep emotional connection, fostering patience, trust, and resilience.

Example:

1. **Offer a Simple Prayer Together** – Light a diya or incense stick in your home, close your eyes, and take a moment to wish for peace and happiness in your relationship.

2. **Chant a Mantra for Positivity** – Reciting mantras such as *Om Namah Shivaya* or *Om Shanti* can create a peaceful environment.
3. **Meditate as a Couple** – Spend a few quiet moments sitting together, focusing on gratitude and love.
4. **Visit a Temple or Sacred Place** – Even an occasional temple visit can provide a sense of renewal and spiritual grounding.
5. **Express Gratitude to the Divine** – Before sleeping, silently thank the universe for your partner and the love you share.

A Real-Life Perspective:

Meera and Rohan, married for six years, often found themselves caught up in their busy schedules. Stress from work and family responsibilities made it hard for them to find time for each other. On the advice of an elder, they began a simple practice: every morning, before leaving for work, they would fold their hands in prayer and wish for each other's well-being.

At first, it felt like just another routine, but over time, they noticed a shift in their relationship. This small act **reminded them daily of their commitment, deepened their understanding, and helped them navigate conflicts with more patience and kindness**.

Lesson: A small spiritual practice can bring a sense of togetherness and reinforce the love between partners.

Ways to Bring Spirituality into Your Marriage:

Start the Day with a Blessing – Before stepping out, take a moment to wish each other success and happiness.
Observe Fasting or Rituals Together – If fasting (*vrat*) is a part of your tradition, doing it together can create a shared experience of

devotion.

Light a Diya in the Evening – A simple act of lighting a lamp at dusk and praying for peace can strengthen your emotional bond.

Read a Meaningful Verse Together – Take a moment to reflect on a passage from the Bhagavad Gita, Ramayana, or another spiritual text and discuss its relevance in your marriage.

Send Good Intentions for Each Other – Even if you don't pray together, silently sending love and positive thoughts for your spouse can have a powerful effect.

Final Thought:

A strong marriage is built on love, trust, and mutual respect. When couples nurture their relationship not just emotionally and physically but also spiritually, they create a **foundation of inner peace and deep connection**. Spirituality can be a guiding force, helping partners **stay united through life's ups and downs**.

Your Challenge: Take a small spiritual step today—light a diya, say a kind prayer for your partner, or simply express gratitude. Let this moment bring you closer.

WEEK 2: STRENGTHENING EMOTIONAL CONNECTION

Day 8 : Love in Their Language - Speak Their Heart

Day 9 : Words of Affirmation - Speak Encouragement

Day 10 : Eliminate Distractions- Be Fully Present

Day 11 : Express Gratitude - Acknowledge Unseen

Day 12 : Apologize First - Take Responsibility

Day 13 : Show Physical Affection - Power of Touch

Day 14 : Laughter Therapy - Add Joy into Marriage

DAY 8: LOVE IN THEIR LANGUAGE – SPEAK THEIR HEART'S DIALECT

Express love in the way your spouse wants.

Sanskrit Wisdom:

"Sarve bhavantu sukhinah."

"May everyone be happy and at peace." – Brihadaranyaka Upanishad 1.4.14

Love is not a rigid formula; it is a flowing river that takes different shapes depending on the person receiving it. In Indian traditions, expressions of love vary widely—some use affectionate words, while others show love through small thoughtful gestures, shared time, or acts of care.

A loving relationship thrives when both partners understand **how the other feels most valued**. Just as the sacred rivers of India take different paths but all nourish life, love too must be **expressed in a way that reaches the heart of your spouse**.

Take the example of **Lord Rama and Sita**. Rama, bound by duty, could not always express his emotions in words, yet his unwavering commitment to Sita spoke volumes. Sita, in return, demonstrated love through **selfless service and loyalty**, standing by his side through exile and hardship. Their love was not based on mere words but on deep mutual understanding.

Similarly, in our daily lives, we often assume that love is felt the same way by everyone. However, one partner might appreciate **verbal expressions of love**, while the other may feel most cherished through **acts of service or quality time**. Recognizing and adapting to these preferences can **transform a marriage into a deeply fulfilling partnership**.

Discovering Your Partner's Love Language:

Love is expressed in different ways. Below are some ways to identify what makes your spouse feel most appreciated:

Words of Affirmation – Love Through Encouragement
Some people feel loved when they receive heartfelt compliments, appreciation, and kind words. Simple expressions of admiration can uplift them.
Example: Instead of a general *"I love you,"* say *"I admire the way you take care of our family"* or *"Your kindness makes our home so warm and beautiful."*

Acts of Service – Love Through Actions

For many, love is best demonstrated through thoughtful actions rather than words. Cooking a meal, fixing something around the house, or running an errand can mean more than a grand declaration of love.

Example: If your spouse values actions, take a task off their plate —perhaps by preparing their favorite meal or handling a chore they usually do.

Quality Time – Love Through Presence
Some people feel most connected when they spend uninterrupted time with their loved one. It's not about expensive outings but about **being mentally and emotionally present**.

Example: Set aside time to take an evening walk together, have tea on the balcony without distractions, or just sit and share thoughts at the end of the day.

Thoughtful Gifts – Love Through Tokens of Affection
In Indian culture, gifts have always been a way of expressing love —whether it's a simple flower, a homemade sweet, or a surprise

note tucked into a lunchbox. The effort behind the gift is what truly matters.
Example: If your spouse loves gifts, bring home a small token of love—a favorite snack, a meaningful book, or a handwritten note.

Physical Touch – Love Through Warmth and Closeness
A gentle touch on the shoulder, holding hands, or a warm hug after a long day can communicate love in ways words cannot. Many people feel emotionally reassured through physical closeness.
Example: Hold hands while watching a movie, offer a reassuring pat when they are stressed, or simply sit close during conversations.

A Story of Realization:
Aditi and Rohan had been married for five years, but Rohan often felt that Aditi didn't acknowledge his efforts. He would surprise her with expensive gifts, yet she rarely seemed excited. One day, Aditi shared, *"I don't need gifts. I just want us to sit together and talk."*

Rohan realized that while **he expressed love through gifts, Aditi valued quality time**. He made an effort to spend time with her every evening, listening to her thoughts without distractions. In return, Aditi started appreciating his thoughtful gestures more. Their marriage transformed not by **grand actions but by understanding what truly made each other feel loved**.

How to Identify Your Spouse's Love Language:

Observe: Notice how they show love to you—it often reflects how they wish to receive love.
Ask: Have an open discussion about what makes them feel most loved.
Experiment: Try different approaches and see what makes them

light up the most.
Listen to Their Complaints: If they frequently say, *"You never listen to me"* or *"We never spend time together,"* that's a clue to what they value most.

Final Thought:

Love is **not about how you want to express it—it's about how your partner truly feels it**. By understanding your spouse's love language, you **deepen your connection, reduce misunderstandings, and create a relationship built on genuine appreciation**.

Your Challenge: Today, express love in your spouse's preferred way—whether through words, time, actions, gifts, or touch. Observe how their face lights up when they receive love in a way that resonates with their heart.

DAY 9: WORDS OF AFFIRMATION – SPEAK ENCOURAGEMENT
Compliment your spouse sincerely today.

Ancient Wisdom:
"Vacham kurvantu madhuram."
"Let your words be sweet and kind." – Atharva Veda 6.8.3

The Power of Words in a Relationship

Words can either heal or harm. They have the ability to create closeness or build walls. In a marriage, the way we speak to our spouse directly impacts the emotional atmosphere of the relationship. Encouraging words **validate efforts, boost confidence, and reassure love**.

In Indian culture, **speech is considered sacred**—it is believed that words, when spoken with sincerity, carry energy and influence destiny. This is why **mantras and prayers are recited with reverence**. Similarly, in a marriage, the way partners communicate can strengthen or weaken their bond.

Think about a time someone's words uplifted you when you were struggling—**didn't it give you strength?** Now, imagine offering that same emotional support to your spouse every day.

Why Encouraging Words Matter in Marriage

They Strengthen the Bond: Verbal appreciation makes a person feel valued.
They Uplift During Difficult Times: When your spouse is struggling, a few words of encouragement can help them push through.
They Create an Emotionally Safe Space: A home filled with kind

words becomes a place of comfort and love.

A Story from Indian History: The Supportive Words of a Queen

In ancient India, **Rani Chennamma of Kittur** was one of the first female warriors to stand against British rule. But behind her fearless leadership was the unwavering support of her husband, Raja Mallasarja. He always reminded her of her strength and intelligence, ensuring she never doubted her own abilities. His encouragement played a key role in shaping her confidence, which later helped her lead her people with courage.

This teaches us that **a spouse's words have the power to ignite determination and self-belief**. When you express admiration and appreciation for your partner, you contribute to their inner strength.

Ways to Use Words of Encouragement in Your Relationship

Express Gratitude for Everyday Efforts
Example: Instead of assuming they know you appreciate them, say it out loud:
"I love that you always remember to make tea for me—it's a small thing, but it means a lot."

Compliment Their Strengths and Personality

Example: Go beyond physical compliments and acknowledge their character:
"Your patience with the kids is incredible. I really admire how much love and effort you put into our family."

Encourage Their Dreams and Goals

Example: Support their ambitions by believing in them:
"I know you're nervous about the new project, but I've seen how

capable you are. You're going to do amazing!"

Comfort Them in Tough Moments

Example: When your spouse is feeling low, remind them of their strength:
"I see how hard you're working. No matter what happens, I'm here for you, and I believe in you."

Use Their Name Affectionately
Names hold emotional significance. When spoken with love, they deepen the impact of the message.

Example: Instead of a generic compliment, make it personal:
"Aditi, I love how your kindness makes everyone around you feel at home. You truly have a beautiful heart."

A Simple Habit to Strengthen Your Bond

Challenge for the Day: Give your spouse one genuine compliment today. Whether through a text, a note, or face-to-face, **let them hear your appreciation**.
Example:
Text Message: *"Thinking of you and just wanted to say how much I admire your patience and kindness."*
Sticky Note: *"You inspire me every day with your dedication and love!"*

Final Thought:

Love is not just about big gestures—it's about the **consistent words of appreciation that remind your spouse they are loved, admired, and valued.**

What words of encouragement will you share with your spouse today?

DAY 10: ELIMINATE DISTRACTIONS – BE FULLY PRESENT

Today give your spouse full attention.

Sanskrit Wisdom:

"Ekagram manah krtva."

"Focus your mind on one thing." – Bhagavad Gita 6.14

The Gift of Undivided Attention

In our daily routines, we often find ourselves preoccupied —scrolling through our phones, mentally drafting work emails, or multitasking while our spouse speaks. While these habits might seem harmless, over time, they create emotional distance.

One of the most powerful ways to strengthen a relationship is to **be fully present when your partner is with you**. Giving them your complete attention sends a silent but profound message: **"You are important to me."**

In Indian traditions, mindfulness has always been a key aspect of deep connections—whether in spiritual practices, family interactions, or relationships. A simple yet impactful way to nurture love is by eliminating distractions and engaging fully in the present moment with your spouse.

A Lesson from Ancient Wisdom: The Power of Presence

Think about two different scenarios:

- A couple sitting together—one is lost in their phone while the other talks. Although they share the same space, they are emotionally disconnected.

- Another couple, where one looks into the other's eyes, listens with care, and responds with warmth. Even if they speak for just five minutes, the connection deepens.

This is the power of being truly present.

Ancient stories illustrate this idea beautifully. When Lord Rama and Sita were in exile, despite the challenges of the forest, Rama was attentive to Sita's needs, making her feel secure and cherished. Their time together was not defined by luxury but by presence and devotion.

In contrast, Ravana, despite his power and wealth, failed to understand or genuinely connect with Sita, which led to his downfall. This highlights that **true connection is not about material wealth but about how deeply we engage with those we love.**

Ways to Be Fully Present in Your Relationship

Create Distraction-Free Moments
Example: Set aside a specific time each day—like during meals or before bed—where both of you put your phones away and talk without interruptions.
Listen with Intent
Example: When your spouse speaks, look into their eyes, nod in understanding, and respond thoughtfully instead of giving half-hearted replies.
Be Emotionally Attentive
Example: Instead of mentally planning what you'll say next, focus entirely on understanding their words and emotions.
□ **Turn Everyday Activities into Quality Time**
Example: Whether drinking tea together or driving somewhere, make those moments count by truly engaging with each other.

Greet Each Other with Presence
Example: When your spouse comes home or wakes up, take a moment to smile, ask about their day, and show genuine warmth before jumping into tasks or distractions.

Today's Challenge: Try a 30-Minute Distraction Detox

For the next 30 minutes, give your spouse undivided attention. Whether it's a conversation, a walk, or just sitting together, let them feel that they have all of you.

What small change will you make today to be more present in your relationship?

DAY 11: EXPRESS GRATITUDE – ACKNOWLEDGE THE UNSEEN

Thank them today for something often unnoticed.

Sanskrit Wisdom:

"Yatha pinde tatha brahmande."

"As is the microcosm, so is the macrocosm." – Yajur Veda

The Power of Gratitude in Relationships

In daily life, we often overlook the little things our spouse does for us. Whether it's ensuring meals are ready, offering emotional support, or taking care of responsibilities without being asked, these small yet significant acts shape a loving relationship. **Acknowledging these efforts strengthens your bond and nurtures appreciation in your marriage.**

In Indian culture, gratitude is deeply woven into traditions. Many families express thanks before meals, recognizing not just the food but also the efforts that went into preparing it. Similarly, when we consciously express appreciation for our spouse's contributions, we create a more fulfilling and harmonious relationship.

A Story of Silent Dedication

Consider the story of a wife who wakes up before dawn to prepare breakfast for her family, ensuring everyone starts the day well. Or a husband who, after a long day at work, still makes time to listen and be present for his partner. Neither expects recognition, yet their actions speak of deep love and commitment.

In the Ramayana, Hanuman selflessly served Lord Rama without seeking praise. His devotion was unwavering, whether he was delivering Rama's message to Sita or carrying the Sanjeevani mountain to save Lakshmana. **His efforts were eventually acknowledged, and that recognition meant more than any reward.** Similarly, your spouse's quiet contributions deserve acknowledgment, no matter how small they seem.

Recognizing Everyday Acts of Love

Appreciate the Little Things
Example: Instead of assuming household chores are routine, thank your spouse for making meals, managing bills, or keeping things organized.
Acknowledge Emotional Support
Example: If they always lend a listening ear when you need to vent, let them know how much it means to you.
Recognize Their Hard Work
Example: If they adjust their schedule for family needs or work hard to provide, express your appreciation in words and actions.
Show Gratitude Through Gestures
Example: If they always serve you tea or coffee, surprise them by doing the same for them.

Today's Task: A Simple 'Thank You' with Meaning

Pick one thing your spouse does regularly but rarely gets acknowledgment for.

Look them in the eyes and say, "I truly appreciate this. Thank you for everything you do."

Small words, spoken sincerely, can leave a lasting impact. How will you express gratitude today?

DAY 12: APOLOGIZE FIRST – TAKE RESPONSIBILITY

If a fight happens today, apologize first for your part

Sanskrit Wisdom:

"Kshama virasya bhushanam."

"Forgiveness is the ornament of the brave." – Mahabharata

Every relationship faces moments of disagreement, but what truly defines its strength is how quickly those conflicts are resolved. Holding onto pride can create emotional distance, whereas apologizing first can bring hearts closer together. Contrary to popular belief, saying "I'm sorry" is not a sign of weakness—it reflects emotional strength, humility, and a commitment to love.

In Indian traditions, the quality of *kshama* (forgiveness) is considered a great virtue. Just as we seek forgiveness from the divine for our mistakes, we should also extend the same grace to our loved ones. Apologizing first doesn't mean admitting full fault —it means valuing the relationship over the argument.

A Lesson from Lord Krishna's Humility

In our mythology, even the most powerful beings show the importance of humility. Lord Krishna, despite his wisdom and strength, never hesitated to offer words of reassurance or peace when misunderstandings arose. Whether calming Arjuna's doubts on the battlefield or diffusing tense situations with his diplomacy, Krishna always prioritized relationships over pride.

Similarly, in marriage, small misunderstandings can escalate when neither partner wants to back down. But taking the first step towards peace can prevent unnecessary pain.

Why Apologizing First Strengthens Love

It Breaks the Cycle of Ego
Clinging to pride only deepens resentment. A heartfelt apology helps both partners move forward.
It Shows Commitment to the Relationship
Saying sorry first signals that you value your bond more than "winning" the argument.
It Opens the Door to Honest Communication
Apologies create a safe space where both partners can express their feelings freely.
It Sets a Positive Example
In families, children often mirror their parents' behavior. Demonstrating humility teaches them the power of reconciliation.

How to Apologize with Sincerity

Use Words That Heal
Avoid generic phrases like “Fine, I’m sorry.” Instead, try: “I realize I hurt you, and I deeply regret it. Let’s talk.”
Own Your Actions Without Shifting Blame
An apology should focus on your role in the situation. Instead of "I’m sorry, but you also..." say, "I regret how I reacted."
Back Up Your Apology with Actions
If the argument stemmed from forgetfulness, be more mindful next time. Show through actions that you are making an effort.

Today's Task: Take the First Step

If you and your spouse have had a disagreement, be the first to reach out. Even if you believe both of you contributed to the issue, acknowledge your part and express a willingness to make things right.

Try saying: *"I love you more than this argument. I'm sorry for my part, and I want us to move forward together."*

Choosing love over ego is a mark of true emotional wisdom. Who will you choose today—your pride or your relationship?

DAY 13: SHOW PHYSICAL AFFECTION – THE POWER OF TOUCH
Hold hands, hug or cuddle.

Sanskrit Wisdom:
"Samsara sagare magnaḥ sneha pashena baddhyate."
"In the vast ocean of life, love is the bond that holds us together." – Mahabharata

---

Love Beyond Words: The Silent Language of Touch

Love isn't just about spoken expressions—it is also conveyed through touch. A reassuring pat on the back, an affectionate squeeze of the hand, or a warm embrace after a long day can communicate what words sometimes fail to express.

In Indian families, affection is often displayed subtly, yet its impact is profound. The gentle touch of a mother's hand on a child's head, an elder's blessing in the form of a tap on the shoulder, or a couple walking hand in hand—all these gestures carry an emotional depth that strengthens bonds.

Studies show that physical affection releases oxytocin, known as the "love hormone," which fosters trust, eases stress, and creates a deep sense of emotional security between partners.

A Lesson from Rama and Sita: Love Through Presence
The legendary love of Rama and Sita teaches us that physical closeness isn't about grand displays but about providing silent strength. During their exile in the forest, they had no luxuries, yet their love flourished in the simplicity of their togetherness.

Whether it was walking side by side in the woods or sharing warmth during the cold nights, their presence alone became their greatest source of comfort.

This reminds us that love is not about extravagant gestures but in the small, meaningful moments of closeness we share daily.

Why Physical Affection Matters in Marriage

It Strengthens Emotional Bonds

A simple touch reinforces love and reassures your spouse that they are valued.

It Eases Stress and Increases Happiness

Holding hands or hugging releases feel-good hormones that calm the mind and body.

It Bridges Emotional Distance

If there's been tension or a misunderstanding, physical touch can act as a silent apology and a step toward reconnection.

It Makes Love Tangible

Sometimes, no words are needed—a comforting embrace can express deep care and understanding.

Ways to Show Physical Affection Daily

Hold Hands

Whether at home or outside, holding hands creates an instant sense of closeness.

Give a Warm Hug

A heartfelt hug after a long day can be more comforting than any words of reassurance.

Sit Close Together

Instead of being at a distance, lean in while sitting together to build a natural connection.

Offer a Gentle Touch

A light touch on the shoulder, a back rub, or running your fingers through their hair can be small yet powerful gestures of love.

Morning & Night Rituals

Start and end the day with a moment of affection—whether it's a warm hug in the morning or holding hands before bedtime.

Today's Task: Make a Loving Gesture

Take a moment today to show physical affection in a way that feels natural and meaningful. Surprise your spouse with a warm embrace, hold their hand while talking, or simply rest your head on their shoulder. These simple acts can make a world of difference.

Try saying: *"I just want to hold you for a moment."* or *"Your hugs make everything feel better."*

Love isn't just heard—it's felt. How will you make your spouse feel loved today?

DAY 14: LAUGHTER THERAPY : ADD JOY INTO YOUR MARRIAGE

Share joyful moments.

Ancient Wisdom:

"Anando hi param lakshyam."

"True happiness is the ultimate goal." – Vedic Teachings

The Power of Laughter in Strengthening Your Bond

Laughter is a natural stress reliever and a powerful way to keep your relationship lighthearted and full of joy. It bridges emotional gaps, diffuses tension, and strengthens intimacy. A marriage should not only be about responsibilities and routines—it should also be filled with moments of shared joy and silliness.

When couples laugh together, they cultivate a relationship that is both resilient and fulfilling. A simple joke, a funny memory, or playful teasing can turn an ordinary day into something special.

T

hink of a moment when you and your spouse laughed so hard that tears welled up in your eyes. Those instances are reminders of why humor is such a vital ingredient in love—it makes the relationship feel fresh, easy, and deeply connected.

A Lesson from Krishna's Playfulness

Lord Krishna, known for his divine wisdom, was also playful and mischievous. His lighthearted nature brought happiness to those around him, reminding us that joy is essential even in the most challenging times.

In relationships, a similar approach can be beneficial. When life gets overwhelming, a shared laugh can ease the pressure and remind you both of the simple happiness of being together.

Why Laughter is Essential in a Relationship

Deepens Emotional Connection

Shared humor builds an unbreakable bond and creates fond memories.

Eases Stress and Relieves Tension

A lighthearted approach makes tough situations feel more manageable.

Encourages Openness and Comfort

Couples who laugh together feel more at ease and secure with each other.

Adds Fun and Spontaneity

Playfulness prevents the relationship from feeling monotonous.

Creates a Positive Atmosphere

Couples who find joy in everyday moments cultivate a happier home.

Ways to Add More Laughter to Your Marriage

Watch Something Funny Together

Pick a comedy film, stand-up special, or viral video to enjoy together.

Reminisce About Funny Memories

Talk about a hilarious moment you both experienced and relive the joy.

Have Playful Conversations

Engage in light teasing, playful banter, or even silly voices to keep things fun.

Turn Mistakes into Laughter

Instead of getting frustrated over small mishaps, laugh them off and move on.

Do Something Unpredictable

Dance in the kitchen, make funny faces, or try a fun game together.

Today's Task: Spark Joy in Your Spouse's Day

Find a way to make your spouse laugh today—it could be through a joke, a shared memory, or a playful moment.

Try saying: *"Do you remember the time we...?"* or *"You always make me laugh when you..."*

A relationship filled with joy is a relationship that thrives. So, what will you do today to bring a smile to your partner's face?

WEEK 3: DEEPENING TRUST AND RESPECT

Day 15: Keep Promises – Strengthen Trust Through Commitment

Day 16: Be Transparent – Strengthen Trust Through Honesty

Day 17: Admit Mistakes – Strengthen Your Bond with Accountability

Day 18: Trust Through Actions – Build Reliability in Everyday Moments

Day 19: Foster Openess- Keep No Secrets

Day 20 : Honor Each Other's Uniqunesss - Respect Differences

Day 21 : Be Their Biggest Supporter- Encourage Their Dreams

DAY 15: KEEP PROMISES – STRENGTHEN TRUST THROUGH COMMITMENT

Today honor your commitment.

Ancient Wisdom:

"Satyam eva jayate."

"Truth alone prevails." – Mundaka Upanishad 3.1.6

A promise is more than just words—it's a reflection of your integrity and love. In a marriage, keeping your word builds trust and reassures your partner that they can rely on you. Whether it's a simple commitment like being home on time or a larger vow to support each other through life's ups and downs, honoring promises strengthens the bond between spouses.

On the other hand, broken promises, even small ones, can create disappointment and weaken the foundation of trust. Consistently following through on your commitments shows your spouse that you value and respect them.

A Lesson from Lord Rama's Devotion to His Word

In ancient Indian history, Lord Rama is revered for his steadfast commitment to his word. Despite the hardships it brought, he honored his father's promise, showcasing the importance of integrity and responsibility.

In marriage, being reliable in small and big ways reassures your spouse that your words carry meaning. Trust is not built in a day but through repeated actions that prove your dependability.

Why Keeping Promises Matters in Marriage

Strengthens Trust

When you consistently keep your word, your spouse knows they can count on you.

Shows Respect

Honoring commitments demonstrates that your partner's feelings and time are important to you.

Deepens Emotional Connection

A dependable partner fosters a safe and loving environment.

Prevents Misunderstandings

Failing to keep promises can lead to frustration and miscommunication.

Reflects Your Character

Integrity is about ensuring your actions align with your words.

Practical Ways to Honor Your Promises

✓ **Make Promises Thoughtfully**

Only commit to things you genuinely intend to follow through on.

✓ **Take Action Immediately**

Don't postpone commitments—act on them as soon as possible.

✓ **Communicate When Plans Change**

If you're unable to keep a promise, inform your spouse and make alternate arrangements.

✓ **Set Reminders for Important Dates**

Use notes or digital reminders to avoid forgetting significant commitments.

✓ **Let Your Actions Speak**

Consistency is key—proving reliability through actions is more powerful than words alone.

Today's Task: Strengthen Trust with a Kept Promise

Reflect on a promise you made to your spouse—big or small—and fulfill it today.

Try saying: *"I remember promising this to you, and I want to show you that I mean what I say."*

A strong relationship is built on trust, and trust is reinforced through action. What promise will you keep today? ❤

DAY 16: BE TRANSPARENT – STRENGTHEN TRUST THROUGH HONESTY

Share your thoughts and feelings openly.

Timeless Wisdom:

"Na hi satyen puthitam kinchana."

"There is nothing greater than truthfulness." – Mahabharata 12.329.13

A thriving marriage is built on trust, and trust flourishes when there is open and honest communication. Sharing your thoughts, emotions, and concerns with your spouse fosters a deeper connection and prevents misunderstandings. Keeping feelings bottled up or avoiding important conversations can create emotional distance and resentment over time.

Transparency does not mean saying everything that comes to mind without thought; it means being truthful while also being kind and considerate. When both partners feel safe to express themselves without fear of judgment, their bond strengthens, and their love deepens.

Learning from Krishna's Wisdom

Lord Krishna was known for his clarity in communication. When guiding Arjuna in his moment of doubt, he spoke with wisdom and sincerity, providing the truth in a way that enlightened rather than hurt. In relationships, truth should be expressed with the same level of care—honestly but with love and understanding.
Just as Krishna's guidance helped Arjuna find clarity, openness in marriage allows both partners to understand and support each

other better.

How Transparency Strengthens Your Relationship

❤ **Fosters Trust**

When you are honest with your spouse, it reassures them that they can rely on you completely.

❤ **Prevents Misunderstandings**

Open communication eliminates assumptions and confusion.

❤ **Deepens Emotional Intimacy**

Sharing thoughts and feelings creates a strong emotional bond.

❤ **Encourages Growth as a Couple**

When both partners are open, they work together to build a stronger future.

❤ **Strengthens Respect**

Being truthful in a kind manner shows that you respect your partner and value the relationship.

Ways to Practice Openness in Your Marriage

✓ **Communicate Your Feelings**

Express what's on your mind calmly and openly instead of suppressing emotions.

✓ **Be a Safe Space for Your Spouse**

Encourage them to share their thoughts without fear of criticism or dismissal.

✓ **Speak with Kindness**

Honesty should always come with empathy—choose words that uplift rather than hurt.

✓ **Acknowledge Mistakes**

If you make an error, own up to it instead of hiding or making excuses.

✓ **Have Regular Check-ins**

Set aside time to talk about your relationship and ensure both of you feel heard.

Today's Challenge: Share a Truth with Your Spouse

Take a moment to be completely open about something that's been on your mind. Whether it's a personal goal, an emotion, or a small concern, start a conversation that deepens your connection.

Try saying: *"I want us to always be honest with each other. Here's something I've been thinking about..."*

A marriage built on openness stands the test of time. What truth will you share today? ❤

DAY 17: ADMIT MISTAKES – STRENGTHEN YOUR BOND WITH ACCOUNTABILITY

Acknowledge when you are wrong.

Timeless Wisdom:

"Kshama virasya bhushanam."

"Forgiveness is the adornment of the courageous." – Mahabharata

---

Every relationship has its ups and downs, and mistakes are a natural part of any journey together. However, what truly matters is how we respond when we realize we've erred. Taking responsibility for our actions strengthens trust, fosters mutual respect, and brings emotional closeness.

A sincere apology does more than just mend the present—it paves the way for a healthier future. Owning up to a mistake shows emotional intelligence and reassures your spouse that honesty and growth are at the heart of your marriage. In contrast, avoiding accountability can create distance and resentment.

When you admit an error with sincerity, your partner sees your willingness to grow, which in turn encourages open communication and a deeper connection.

A Lesson from Yudhishthira: The Power of Responsibility

Yudhishthira, revered for his righteousness, was not without faults. His decision to gamble away his kingdom and family was a grave mistake, yet instead of blaming others, he accepted responsibility. His humility did not make him weak—it earned him greater respect and loyalty.

In marriage, acknowledging faults is not a sign of defeat; it is a sign of strength. When both partners are willing to be accountable, it cultivates a relationship built on trust and understanding.

Why Taking Responsibility Strengthens Relationships

❤ **Builds Trust**
Acknowledging mistakes reassures your spouse of your honesty.

❤ **Prevents Unspoken Resentment**
Openly admitting faults stops small misunderstandings from becoming big issues.

❤ **Encourages Growth**
Learning from past actions helps both individuals evolve in the relationship.

❤ **Creates a Safe Emotional Space**
When one person admits fault, it fosters an environment where both can be vulnerable.

❤ **Deepens Emotional Connection**
Transparency and humility bring couples closer together.

How to Practice Accountability in Marriage

✓ **Pause and Reflect**
Instead of reacting defensively, take a moment to assess the situation honestly.

✓ **Apologize with Sincerity**
A simple, heartfelt "I was wrong, and I'm sorry" has the power to heal wounds.

✓ **Listen Without Defensiveness**
Understand how your actions impacted your spouse and validate their feelings.

✓ **Take Steps to Improve**
Actions speak louder than words—show that you're committed to change.

✓ **Encourage Open Communication**
When both partners feel safe to admit mistakes, it leads to a

stronger, more understanding relationship.

Today's Challenge: Take Ownership of a Mistake

Think about a recent disagreement or moment where you could have handled things better. Approach your spouse and acknowledge it honestly.

Try saying: *"I realize I was wrong when I did/said ___. I truly regret it, and I'll do better next time."*

A strong marriage isn't about avoiding mistakes—it's about how you work through them together. What step will you take today to strengthen your relationship? ❤

DAY 18: TRUST THROUGH ACTIONS – BUILD RELIABILITY IN EVERYDAY MOMENTS

Show reliability in small things.

Ancient Wisdom:

"Kartavyam yoginah sada."

"One must always fulfill their duties with sincerity." – Bhagavad Gita 3.20

Trust is Shaped by Actions, Not Just Words

In a marriage, trust isn't something that happens overnight—it grows through consistency. The little things, like remembering a commitment or being there when needed, mean more than grand declarations. Reliability in small matters builds a foundation of trust that strengthens the relationship over time.

When you follow through on what you say, your spouse feels safe and valued. It's not just about avoiding disappointment; it's about proving, day by day, that your words carry weight.

Lessons from Hanuman: Devotion Through Deeds

Hanuman's unwavering dedication to Lord Rama wasn't based on words alone—it was shown in his actions. Whether leaping across the ocean, searching for Sita, or carrying an entire mountain to save Lakshmana, Hanuman never hesitated. His reliability made him one of the most trusted figures in the Ramayana.

Similarly, in marriage, dependability is built through everyday gestures. Being present, keeping commitments, and taking responsibility—even for minor things—nurture a sense of security in your bond.

Why Dependability Strengthens Marriage

❤ **Fosters Emotional Security**

When your spouse knows they can rely on you, they feel reassured and at peace.

❤ **Strengthens Mutual Respect**

Consistently keeping your word shows integrity and deepens respect.

❤ **Reduces Stress in Daily Life**

When both partners fulfill their responsibilities, life runs more smoothly.

❤ **Deepens Emotional Intimacy**

Trust builds closeness, making it easier to share feelings and vulnerabilities.

Simple Ways to Show You're Reliable

✓ **Be On Time**

Whether it's for a conversation, a date, or a simple favor, showing up when promised strengthens trust.

✓ **Keep Your Word**

If you promise to do something—whether it's fixing something at home or making time to talk—follow through.

✓ **Take Initiative**

Instead of waiting to be asked, step in and help. Whether it's household chores or emotional support, be proactive.

✓ **Check In Regularly**

A simple message asking, *"How's your day going?"* or remembering an important detail about your spouse's schedule shows care.

✓ **Be Consistent**

Reliability isn't about one-time gestures—it's a daily habit that strengthens your relationship over time.

Today's Challenge: Show Your Dependability

Find one way to demonstrate reliability today. It could be completing a task your spouse mentioned, remembering something important to them, or simply being there when they need support.

Try saying: *"I want you to know that you can always count on me, not just in words, but in actions."*

Trust isn't built through promises alone—it's created through consistent, thoughtful actions. How will you prove your reliability today? ❤

DAY 19: FOSTER OPENNESS – KEEP NO SECRETS

Build a culture of openness.

Ancient Wisdom:

"Yo no hanti sa nah priyaḥ."
"One who does not deceive is dear to us." – Rig Veda 8.31.8

Honesty and Transparency Strengthens Love

True intimacy in a relationship is built on trust, and trust thrives in an atmosphere of openness. When partners communicate openly—whether about feelings, finances, or dreams—it deepens their bond and strengthens their connection. However, secrecy can create distance, misunderstandings, and even resentment.

Being transparent does not mean sharing every fleeting thought but ensuring that important aspects of life are discussed honestly. Whether it's a worry about the future, a financial decision, or an emotional concern, open communication helps couples navigate life together in harmony.

A Lesson from the Ramayana

The epic Ramayana teaches a powerful lesson about the consequences of hidden intentions. Queen Kaikeyi's decision to secretly demand Lord Rama's exile created heartbreak in the kingdom. Had she communicated her fears and desires openly, the pain and suffering of her family might have been avoided.
Similarly, in relationships, unspoken concerns or concealed truths can lead to unnecessary conflict. True partnership thrives when both individuals feel safe to share openly without fear of judgment.

Why Transparency Matters in Marriage

❤ **Strengthens Trust**
When you're open with your spouse, they feel valued and secure.
❤ **Fosters Emotional Intimacy**
Sharing your thoughts and emotions deepens your connection.
❤ **Reduces Misunderstandings**
Many conflicts arise from assumptions or lack of communication. Honesty helps clear doubts before they turn into issues.
❤ **Encourages Teamwork**
A marriage flourishes when both partners are aligned in their goals, choices, and expectations.

Ways to Cultivate Openness in Your Relationship

✓ **Be Honest About Finances**
Money matters can be a source of stress. Discuss expenses, savings, and financial goals together.
✓ **Communicate Future Aspirations**
Talk about career plans, personal growth, and long-term dreams to ensure you both feel included in each other's journey.
✓ **Express Your Feelings Freely**
If something is troubling you, share it calmly instead of bottling it up. Your spouse can only support you if they know how you feel.
✓ **Admit Mistakes with Honesty**
If you've made an error, own up to it rather than hiding it. Taking responsibility strengthens respect.
✓ **Create a Safe Space for Conversations**
Encourage open discussions where both partners feel heard, without fear of criticism or judgment.

Today's Challenge: Have a Heartfelt Conversation

Find a quiet moment today and share something meaningful with your spouse—whether it's an aspiration, a concern, or an emotion you've been keeping to yourself.

Try saying: *"I value our relationship and want us to always be honest with each other. Is there anything on your mind that you'd like to share?"*

A relationship built on trust and transparency is one that stands the test of time. How will you bring more openness into your marriage today? ❤

DAY 20: HONOR EACH OTHER'S UNIQUENESS- RESPECT DIFFERENCES

Accept your spouse's individuality.

Timeless Wisdom:

"Vasudhaiva kutumbakam."
"The entire world is one family." – Mahaupanishad 6.71

No two individuals are exactly alike, and that's the beauty of a marriage. A healthy relationship does not require both partners to think, act, or feel the same way—it flourishes when both people respect and appreciate each other's uniqueness.

When you embrace your spouse's individuality rather than expecting them to change, you create an environment of mutual understanding and unconditional love. Differences should not be seen as barriers but as opportunities to learn, grow, and expand your perspective.

A Lesson from Krishna and Radha

Krishna and Radha had distinct personalities—Krishna was playful, wise, and charismatic, while Radha embodied deep love and devotion. Despite their differences, they shared a profound connection that was built on mutual admiration and acceptance. Their story reminds us that a strong relationship is not about changing the other person but about cherishing them for who they are.

Why Embracing Differences Strengthens a Relationship

Encourages Growth – When you accept your spouse's uniqueness, you support their personal and emotional development.
Prevents Unnecessary Conflicts – Understanding that differences are natural reduces misunderstandings and tension.
Fosters Emotional Safety – When someone feels accepted as they are, they feel more secure in the relationship.
Deepens Connection – Appreciating each other's unique traits builds respect and admiration.

Ways to Celebrate Each Other's Individuality

✓ **Encourage Their Interests** – Even if you don't share the same hobbies, support what makes them happy.
✓ **Respect Their Perspective** – Instead of trying to "win" an argument, listen and understand their point of view.
✓ **Give Each Other Space** – Allow room for personal growth while maintaining a strong bond.
✓ **Recognize Their Strengths** – Focus on the qualities that make them special rather than trying to "fix" differences.
✓ **Celebrate What Makes You Different** – Instead of seeing differences as obstacles, view them as ways to balance and complement each other.

Today's Challenge: Acknowledge and Appreciate

Take a moment to notice something unique about your spouse—perhaps a habit, a talent, or a way of thinking that is different from yours but adds value to your relationship.

Try saying: *"I love that you see things differently from me. It makes our life together more interesting and complete."*

A fulfilling marriage is built on love that honors individuality. How will you celebrate your spouse's uniqueness today? ❤

DAY 21: BE THEIR BIGGEST SUPPORTER – ENCOURAGE THEIR DREAMS

Encourage your spouse's personal growth.

Ancient Wisdom:

"Udhyamam saṁpadam kṛtvā."

"Success is achieved through effort." – Bhagavad Gita 18.46

Strengthening Love Through Encouragement

A thriving relationship isn't just about sharing love—it's about nurturing growth. Supporting your spouse's aspirations shows that you believe in their potential and are committed to their happiness. When both partners uplift each other, they cultivate a relationship where dreams are not only pursued but celebrated.

The best relationships create a foundation where each person feels inspired to become the best version of themselves. Encouragement, reassurance, and belief in one another fuel confidence and deepen emotional intimacy.

Lessons from Timeless Bonds

Sita and Rama: Sita stood by Rama's side, offering unwavering support as he fulfilled his dharma. Her faith in him never wavered, even in the toughest times.

Krishna and Arjuna: On the battlefield, Krishna reminded Arjuna of his strength and purpose, guiding him toward his true potential. With the right encouragement, Arjuna found the courage to move forward.

These examples teach us that standing by your partner's dreams fosters trust, strength, and deeper love.

How Encouragement Transforms a Relationship

Deepens Trust: Knowing your partner believes in you builds a strong emotional foundation.
Increases Intimacy: Showing genuine interest in their dreams strengthens your bond.
Boosts Confidence: Your support can be the motivation they need to take the next step.
Promotes Growth: A relationship flourishes when both partners grow individually and together.

Ways to Support Your Partner's Dreams

Listen with Interest: Ask about their aspirations, goals, and what excites them.
Offer Encouragement: Simple words like *"I believe in you"* can provide a huge boost.
Help in Practical Ways: Find ways to make their journey easier —whether it's helping with research, offering time, or creating a supportive environment.
Be Patient and Understanding: Success takes time. Stay supportive, even during setbacks.
Celebrate Their Achievements: Acknowledge their progress and express pride in their efforts.

Today's Challenge: Show Your Support

Take a moment to encourage your spouse's dreams today. Ask them how you can support their goals or surprise them with a thoughtful action, such as gifting a book related to their passion or offering words of motivation.

A simple statement like *"I admire your dedication"* can mean the world to them. When you lift your spouse higher, your relationship rises with it. ❤

WEEK 4: STRENGTHENING COMMITMENT AND PASSION

Day 22: Express Love Daily – Keep the Spark Alive

Day 23: Rekindle Romance – Keep the Spark Alive

Day 24: Deepen Your Bond – Prioritize Intimacy

Day 25: Thoughtful Surprises – A Spark of Joy

Day 26 : Plan A Date Night - Strengthen Connect

Day 27 : Celebrate Your Partner- Show Gratitude

Day 28 : Reflect on Your Journey - Reignite Bond

DAY 22: EXPRESS LOVE DAILY – KEEP THE SPARK ALIVE

Show affection through words and actions.

Timeless Wisdom:

"Prema bhaktiḥ parama gatiḥ."

"Love and devotion are the highest paths." – Bhagavata Purana 10.14.8

Love is a Daily Practice

Love is not just about special occasions or grand gestures—it's about the little things we do every day. A heartfelt smile, a kind word, or a thoughtful action can make a significant difference in your relationship. When love is expressed consistently, it strengthens emotional bonds, builds trust, and nurtures a deeper connection.

Think of love like a garden—it thrives when tended to regularly. Ignoring it can cause it to wither, but a little care each day keeps it flourishing.

Lessons from Legendary Love Stories

Krishna and Radha: Their love wasn't just in words but in actions. Krishna's devotion to Radha was reflected in the way he cherished and valued her presence.

Sita and Rama: Despite facing trials, Rama remained deeply committed to Sita. His actions demonstrated his unwavering love, proving that love is about standing by each other through every challenge.

These stories remind us that love is not just about what we say but how we show it through consistent, meaningful actions.

Why Showing Love Every Day Matters

Strengthens Connection: Small gestures help reinforce your bond and make your spouse feel cherished.
Creates Security and Trust: Regular expressions of love provide reassurance and deepen emotional safety.
Prevents Taking Each Other for Granted: Acknowledging your partner's presence and efforts makes them feel valued.
Keeps the Romance Alive: When love is shown daily, it sustains intimacy and joy in the relationship.

Ways to Express Love Every Day

Use Kind Words: Say *"I love you,"* express appreciation, or acknowledge something they do for you.
Show Affection: Hold hands, hug, or offer a comforting touch to create warmth and closeness.
Leave Thoughtful Notes: A short, loving message on a sticky note or a heartfelt text can brighten their day.
Do Something Special: Make their favorite drink, handle a task for them, or surprise them with a simple act of kindness.
Share Joy: Laugh together, reminisce about happy moments, or watch something that brings smiles to both of you.

Today's Challenge: Make Love Visible
Find at least one way to express love today. Whether it's a warm embrace, a sweet message, or an act of kindness, let your spouse feel cherished.

Love isn't just meant to be felt—it's meant to be shown, every single day! ❤

DAY 23: REKINDLE ROMANCE – KEEP THE PASSION BURNING

Do something special together.

Timeless Wisdom:

"Sangacchadhwam samvadadhwam."

"Walk together, speak together in harmony." – Rig Veda 10.191.2

Relationships evolve over time, and while familiarity brings comfort, it can sometimes make romance feel like an afterthought. However, keeping love vibrant requires ongoing effort. Romance isn't just about extravagant gestures —it's about creating meaningful moments that deepen your connection.

Love flourishes when both partners are intentional about keeping the excitement alive, much like tending to a flame to keep it burning bright.

Lessons from Enduring Love Stories

Rama & Sita: Even during their time in the forest, Rama and Sita found joy in each other's presence. Their relationship thrived not because of luxury but because of shared moments and unwavering support.

Krishna & Radha: Their love was playful and full of devotion, proving that joy and spontaneity are key ingredients in a lasting relationship.

These stories remind us that romance isn't about expensive gifts or elaborate plans—it's about making each other feel cherished through thoughtful actions.

Why Keeping Romance Alive Matters

Strengthens Emotional Bonds: Prioritizing romance fosters deeper intimacy and connection.
Breaks Monotony: A little spontaneity adds freshness and excitement to the relationship.
Creates Lasting Memories: The special moments you share today become the cherished memories of tomorrow.
Reaffirms Love and Commitment: Making time for romance shows that you value and appreciate your partner.

Ways to Rekindle Romance

Recreate a Meaningful Memory: Revisit the place of your first date, cook a dish that holds sentimental value, or listen to a song that reminds you of a special time.
Make a Meal Together: Cooking as a team is a fun and intimate way to bond.
Plan a Surprise Date: It doesn't have to be extravagant—a simple picnic, a scenic drive, or a cozy evening at home can be special.
Dance Just Because: Play your favorite romantic song and slow dance in your living room.
Write a Love Note: Leave a heartfelt message in a place where your spouse will find it unexpectedly.
Watch a Romantic Movie: Spend time cuddling and enjoying a film that reminds you of the beauty of love.
Go for a Walk Together: Holding hands and talking about your dreams and memories can reignite emotional closeness.

Today's Challenge: Create a Romantic Moment

Set aside time today to do something meaningful for your partner. Whether it's a heartfelt conversation, a sweet surprise, or simply holding hands while reminiscing about your journey together, make the moment count.

Romance isn't about grand gestures—it's about making your

partner feel special every single day. Keep the spark alive! ❤

DAY 24: DEEPEN YOUR BOND – PRIORITIZE INTIMACY

Foster physical and emotional closeness.

Timeless Wisdom:

"Sneha-pashena baddhyate."

"Love is the bond that unites us." – Mahabharata

The Heart of True Intimacy

A strong marriage isn't just about companionship—it thrives on deep emotional and physical closeness. Intimacy is more than just physical affection; it's about feeling truly connected, valued, and understood by your spouse. It's found in tender moments, meaningful conversations, and the quiet assurance that you are each other's safe space.

Over time, routine and responsibilities can make couples drift into autopilot. That's why consciously nurturing intimacy is essential. A touch, a glance, or a heartfelt conversation can rekindle warmth and reinforce the love that brought you together.

Lessons from Timeless Love Stories

Rama & Sita: Their love endured exile and hardships, yet their emotional connection remained strong, built on unwavering support and understanding.

Krishna & Radha: Their love was beyond physical attraction—it was a deep, soulful connection filled with devotion, laughter, and shared moments of joy.

These legendary couples remind us that true intimacy isn't just about being near each other but being present in each other's lives with love and intention.

Why Intimacy Matters in Marriage

Strengthens Emotional Security: When partners openly express love and affection, they create a safe space for each other.
Deepens Connection: Small gestures of love keep the emotional spark alive.
Boosts Happiness & Well-Being: Acts of affection trigger positive emotions, reducing stress and strengthening the bond.
Reaffirms Commitment: Prioritizing closeness reminds you both of the love and devotion that built your relationship.

Ways to Foster Intimacy in Your Marriage

Make Physical Affection a Habit: Hold hands, hug, or place a reassuring hand on their shoulder—small touches make a big difference.
Have Meaningful Conversations: Go beyond everyday talk—share your thoughts, dreams, and memories to reconnect.
Express Love Through Actions & Words: Leave a heartfelt note, send a sweet message, or simply say, "I appreciate you."
Create Uninterrupted 'Us Time': Set aside distractions and be fully present with each other, whether it's a quiet evening or a shared hobby.
Share Moments of Joy: Dance in the living room, reminisce about your early days, or surprise them with something they love.

Today's Challenge: Make Intimacy a Priority

Take a moment today to nurture intimacy with your spouse. Whether it's through a gentle touch, a loving conversation, or simply enjoying each other's presence, make them feel cherished and valued.

A relationship flourishes when love is continuously nurtured—

invest in your connection and watch it grow. ❤

DAY 25: THOUGHTFUL SURPRISES – A SPARK OF JOY

Bring joy through unexpected gestures.

Ancient Wisdom:

"Yajna dana tapaḥ karma na tyajyam."

"Acts of kindness and love should never be forsaken." – Bhagavad Gita 18.5

A thriving relationship isn't built on grand moments alone—it's nurtured through small, unexpected acts of love. Surprising your spouse with thoughtful gestures keeps the relationship fresh and exciting, reminding them that they are cherished.

It's not about the cost or extravagance; the true essence of a surprise lies in the thought behind it. Whether it's a simple note, an unexpected hug, or an act of service, these small gestures create a deep sense of connection.

Lessons from Timeless Bonds

Krishna's Playfulness: Lord Krishna often delighted his loved ones with unexpected acts of joy, keeping their spirits uplifted.

Rama's Devotion to Sita: Even in the hardships of exile, Rama ensured Sita felt cared for, proving that love is shown through mindful actions.

These stories highlight that love isn't just spoken—it's demonstrated through consistent acts of thoughtfulness.

Why Thoughtful Gestures Matter

Breaks the Routine: Daily responsibilities can make life feel repetitive. A little surprise adds a spark.

Demonstrates Appreciation: It reassures your spouse that they

are always in your thoughts.
Deepens Emotional Bond: Simple acts of kindness create lasting memories and strengthen your connection.
Encourages Gratitude: Thoughtful surprises foster mutual appreciation and joy in the relationship.

Simple Yet Meaningful Ways to Surprise Your Spouse

Leave a Loving Note: Write a heartfelt message and place it where they'll find it—on their pillow, in their bag, or on the bathroom mirror.

Prepare Their Favorite Meal: Cook something special or bring home a treat they love.
Create a Special Moment: Plan an at-home date night, go for a sunset walk, or watch a movie they enjoy.

Give a Small, Meaningful Gift: It could be their favorite snack, a book they've wanted to read, or a playlist of songs that remind you of them.

Do Something Helpful: Take over a task they dislike, whether it's folding laundry, making their morning coffee, or organizing something for them.

Send an Unexpected Message: A random text expressing love and appreciation can brighten their day.

Today's Challenge: Plan a Surprise for Your Spouse

Choose one unexpected way to make your spouse smile today. It doesn't have to be big—just something that says, *"I thought of you."*

Love is best expressed in everyday moments. A thoughtful surprise can turn even an ordinary day into a cherished memory.

❤

DAY 26: PLAN A DATE NIGHT – STRENGTHEN YOUR CONNECTION

Spend quality time without distractions.

Timeless Wisdom:

"Kalayati sarvam."

"Time nurtures all things." – Atharva Veda 19.53.4

Why Spending Quality Time Matters

In the hustle of daily life, it's easy for couples to get caught up in responsibilities and routines, leaving little room for meaningful moments together. But love, like any living thing, needs nourishment. A thoughtfully planned date night is a way to pause, reconnect, and remind each other of the bond you share.

Making time for your partner isn't about grand gestures—it's about showing that your relationship is a priority. Whether it's a quiet evening at home or an adventurous outing, dedicating time exclusively to each other strengthens emotional intimacy.

Lessons from Legendary Love Stories

Krishna & Radha's Cherished Moments: Even with the weight of his divine duties, Krishna always found time to be with Radha, embracing the joy of togetherness.

Rama & Sita's Deep Bond: Despite living in exile, Rama and Sita found solace in each other's presence, proving that true companionship isn't about luxury—it's about connection.

These stories highlight that love isn't measured in extravagant gifts but in shared experiences and heartfelt moments.

Why a Date Night Can Reignite Romance

Fosters Emotional Intimacy: Quality time allows couples to reconnect on a deeper level.
Breaks the Routine: A change of scenery or activity brings excitement and refreshes the relationship.
Creates Beautiful Memories: Special moments together turn into cherished stories that last a lifetime.
Shows Commitment & Care: Taking the time to plan something meaningful demonstrates love and appreciation.

Creative Date Night Ideas

Romantic Dinner: Cook a meal together at home or enjoy a quiet dinner at your favorite restaurant.
Scenic Drive or Walk: Take a long drive, watch the sunset, or go for an evening walk, just the two of you.
Movie or Game Night: Pick a film you both love or play a fun board game for a relaxed evening.
Revisit Special Moments: Look through old photos, reminisce about how you met, or recreate your first date.
Try Something New Together: Whether it's painting, dancing, or baking, a shared activity strengthens connection.
Outdoor Picnic or Stargazing: Escape the routine with a cozy picnic or a peaceful night under the stars.
☕ **Coffee & Conversations:** Visit a café, enjoy your favorite drinks, and have deep, uninterrupted conversations.

Today's Challenge: Make It Special

Plan a dedicated time for just the two of you—free from distractions. It doesn't have to be extravagant; the goal is to be fully present with your spouse.

Love is not just spoken; it's shown through time, attention, and effort. Make today a celebration of your bond! ❤

DAY 27: CELEBRATE YOUR PARTNER – SHOW GRATITUDE FOR THEIR LOVE

Appreciate your spouse's presence in your life.

Wisdom from the Ancients:
"Dhanyaḥ sa jīvan yo premnā jīvati."
"Fortunate is the one who lives with love." – Bhagavad Gita

Why Gratitude Matters in Marriage

Love grows stronger when nurtured with appreciation. In the rhythm of daily life, it's easy to overlook the small yet meaningful things our spouse does. A simple "thank you" or heartfelt recognition can reinforce the foundation of a happy and fulfilling relationship.

Gratitude isn't just about acknowledging big gestures; it's about cherishing the everyday moments—whether it's their unwavering support, patience, or the warmth they bring into your life.

Lessons from Timeless Relationships

Draupadi & the Pandavas: Draupadi's loyalty and sacrifices were deeply valued by the Pandavas, strengthening their relationship through trials and triumphs.

Krishna & Rukmini's Mutual Respect: Rukmini expressed gratitude for Krishna's love, and in return, Krishna honored her devotion, creating a bond of deep understanding and appreciation.

These examples remind us that when we recognize and express gratitude for our partner's presence, love becomes even more meaningful.

How Gratitude Strengthens a Marriage

Creates a Positive Environment: Acknowledging each other's efforts shifts the focus from flaws to blessings.
Deepens Emotional Connection: Genuine appreciation reassures your spouse that they are cherished.
Encourages Thoughtfulness: When people feel valued, they naturally continue to express love and kindness.
Builds Strength During Challenges: Gratitude fosters resilience, making it easier to navigate difficulties as a team.

Ways to Show Appreciation Daily

Write a Heartfelt Note: List the things you love about your spouse and leave it somewhere special.
Speak Your Gratitude: A simple "I appreciate you" can brighten their day.
Surprise Messages: Send an unexpected text or leave a note expressing why you're grateful for them.
Acts of Kindness: Do something thoughtful—make them a meal, help with a task, or offer a comforting gesture.
Gratitude Date Night: Set aside time to reflect on the things you love about each other.
Recognize the Little Things: Appreciate everyday efforts, from their hard work to the love they show in small ways.

Today's Challenge: Express Gratitude to Your Spouse
Take a moment to genuinely acknowledge and appreciate something about your partner. Whether through words, a kind action, or a surprise note, let them know how much they mean to you.

Love thrives on appreciation—nurture it with gratitude! ❤

DAY 28: REFLECT ON YOUR JOURNEY – REIGNITE YOUR COMMITMENT

Strengthen commitment by remembering why you chose each other.

Ancient Wisdom:
"Satatam sampriyam bhavet."
"May love and affection always remain." – Vedic Hymn

The Beauty of Looking Back

Every love story is unique, shaped by moments of joy, growth, and resilience. Over time, couples may get caught up in routines, unintentionally overlooking the beautiful journey they've built together. Taking a step back to reflect on your shared experiences helps reignite appreciation, deepen emotional intimacy, and reinforce the commitment that brought you together.

Your relationship isn't just about where you are now; it's also about where you began and the dreams you continue to build together.

Lessons from Legendary Couples
Rama & Sita: Despite facing exile and hardships, their unwavering support for each other reflected their deep bond.
Krishna & Radha: Though their love transcended the physical world, their connection remained timeless and inspiring.
These stories remind us that relationships flourish when couples cherish their shared experiences and remain committed despite life's uncertainties.

Why Reflection Strengthens Relationships

Reconnects You to Your Roots: Revisiting special memories reminds you why you chose each other.

Fosters Gratitude: Reflecting on challenges you've overcome together builds appreciation for your partner's presence and support.

Encourages Growth: Recognizing how far you've come as a couple allows you to set new goals for the future.

Deepens Emotional Intimacy: Sharing memories strengthens your bond, reigniting the love and connection you share.

Ways to Reflect and Rekindle Love

Browse Through Old Photos: Reminisce about the early days of your relationship, trips you've taken, and milestones you've achieved together.

Revisit Special Messages: Read past love notes, wedding vows, or meaningful texts to relive heartfelt emotions.

Share Your Favorite Moments: Take turns recalling funny, romantic, or unforgettable experiences from your time together.

Recreate a Memorable Date: Revisit a place that holds sentimental value, like where you first met, or cook a favorite meal together.

Write a Love Letter to the Future: Express your gratitude for your partner and your hopes for the future. Open it on a special occasion as a reminder of your journey.

Today's Challenge: Celebrate Your Love Story

Dedicate time today to reflecting on your journey as a couple. Whether it's flipping through old photos, reminiscing over dinner, or simply expressing gratitude for your partner, let today be a reminder of the love that continues to grow between you.

Love is not just about where you're going—it's about cherishing every step along the way. ❤

WEEK 5: CREATING A LASTING LEGACY OF LOVE

Day 29: Share Your Dreams – Build a Future Together

Day 30: Strengthen Financial Unity – Build a Stable Future Together

Day 31: Inspire Through Love – Lead by Example in Your Marriage

Day 32: Strengthen Your Bond Through Service – Serve Together

Day 33: Celebrate Milestones – Honor Your Journey Together

Day 34: Establish Meaningful Traditions – Strengthen Your Bond Through Shared Rituals

Day 35: Embrace Change Together – Navigate Life's Transitions as a Team

DAY 29: SHARE YOUR DREAMS – BUILD A FUTURE TOGETHER

Discuss your vision for the future together.

Sacred Wisdom:

"Saha dharmam chara."

"Walk together in harmony and purpose." – Rig Veda 10.85.42

A strong marriage thrives when both partners not only support each other in the present but also share a vision for the future. Just like a tree grows stronger when its roots are intertwined, a relationship flourishes when couples align their aspirations and walk toward a common goal. Whether it's planning a home, pursuing careers, traveling, or embracing personal growth, discussing dreams strengthens emotional intimacy and deepens commitment.

Dreaming together isn't just about making plans—it's about reinforcing the idea that you are a team, growing side by side, and building a life filled with purpose and love.

Timeless Lessons from Devoted Partnerships

Shiva & Parvati: Their relationship was built on deep conversations about life, purpose, and spiritual growth, strengthening their connection.

Krishna & Rukmini: As partners, they navigated life's challenges together, supporting each other's roles in the grander scheme of dharma and love.

These legendary unions show that discussing the future openly creates a foundation of trust, understanding, and mutual respect.

Why Sharing Your Aspirations Matters

Deepens Emotional Bond: Honest conversations help you understand each other's hopes and desires.

Builds Unity: Knowing where you're headed together prevents misunderstandings and ensures alignment.

Encourages Support & Motivation: When both partners believe in each other's goals, success feels even more rewarding.

Strengthens Commitment: Discussing the future reinforces your dedication to growing together.

Ways to Dream & Plan as a Couple

Create a Shared Vision Board: Gather pictures, words, and symbols that represent the life you both desire—whether it's travel, family, career milestones, or personal growth.

Set Aside Time for Future Talks: Schedule a relaxed evening to discuss short-term and long-term goals, ensuring you're on the same page.

Plan Yearly Milestones: Reflect on past achievements and set new goals—whether they're financial, health-related, or relationship-focused.

Write a Letter to Your Future Selves: Describe your dreams as a couple and revisit the letter in a few years to see how far you've come.

Imagine Your Ideal Life Together: Visualize your dream home, the experiences you want to share, and the values you want to uphold in your marriage.

Today's Challenge: Dream as a Team

Take some time today to openly share your hopes for the future with your spouse. Whether it's something as simple as learning a new skill together or a big goal like relocating, having this conversation will strengthen your bond.

A lasting marriage isn't just about where you are today—it's about where you're heading, hand in hand, with love and intention. ❤

DAY 30: STRENGTHEN FINANCIAL UNITY – ACHEIVE FINANCIAL FREEDOM TOGETHER

Plan your financial future together

Timeless Wisdom:

"Artha eva grihasya mulaṁ."

"Financial stability is the foundation of a household." – Manusmriti 4.8

A successful marriage thrives on trust, communication, and shared responsibilities—including financial well-being. Money matters can either bring a couple closer together or create unnecessary stress. However, when both partners work as a team to manage finances, they build a future that is secure and fulfilling.

Financial unity means making joint decisions, being transparent about earnings and expenses, and planning wisely for both present and future needs. It's not just about wealth—it's about responsible management, mutual understanding, and shared financial goals.

Lessons from Ancient Wisdom

Rama & Sita's Wise Management: Even in exile, Rama and Sita adapted to their circumstances and managed their resources with wisdom, showing that financial discipline is crucial in every stage of life.

Yudhishthira & Draupadi's Resilience: Despite facing financial challenges, they remained committed to responsible decision-making and long-term stability.

These stories highlight that financial security is not about how much one has, but how wisely it is managed together.

Why Financial Transparency is Essential

Reduces Stress & Conflict: Open discussions about money prevent misunderstandings and build mutual trust.
Encourages Teamwork & Accountability: When both partners actively participate in financial decisions, they create a strong foundation for success.
Supports Long-Term Aspirations: Planning together for major milestones—like buying a home, saving for education, or preparing for retirement—ensures a stable future.
Builds Confidence in the Relationship: Honesty about financial matters fosters deeper trust and strengthens the bond between partners.

Practical Ways to Strengthen Financial Unity

Assess Your Financial Situation Together: Review income, expenses, debts, and savings to get a clear picture of where you stand.
Set Joint Financial Goals: Discuss what you both want to achieve —whether it's saving for a trip, paying off a loan, or investing for future security.
Create a Realistic Budget: Allocate funds for necessities, savings, and enjoyment while ensuring financial stability.
Be Honest About Spending: Avoid hiding expenses or making financial decisions without mutual agreement. Transparency is key.
Increase Financial Knowledge Together: Read books, attend financial workshops, or seek expert advice to make informed decisions about saving and investing.

Today's Action Step: Strengthen Financial Alignment

Set aside time today to discuss financial priorities with your spouse. Whether it's reviewing your current expenses, adjusting your savings plan, or setting new goals,
taking this step together will reinforce your partnership.

A financially aligned marriage is not just about managing money —it's about building a future of security, trust, and shared dreams. ❤

DAY 31: INSPIRE THROUGH LOVE – LEAD BY EXAMPLE IN YOUR MARRIAGE

Be a role model for love and harmony.

Timeless Wisdom:
"Yad yad ācarati śreṣṭhas tat tad evetaro janaḥ."
"Whatever a respected person does, others follow." – Bhagavad Gita 3.21

Your Marriage as an Inspiration

A strong and loving marriage doesn't just enrich your own life—it serves as a model for those around you. Your relationship shapes the perceptions of love, respect, and commitment within your family and social circle. Whether it's your children, younger couples, or friends, the way you treat your spouse influences others in ways you may not even realize.

By embodying kindness, patience, and understanding, you create a powerful example of what a healthy, nurturing relationship looks like.

Wisdom from Sacred Unions

Krishna's Leadership: Through his actions and teachings, Krishna set an example of wisdom, responsibility, and love that continues to inspire countless people.

Rama & Sita's Devotion: Despite hardships, their mutual respect and unwavering commitment became a symbol of marital strength and loyalty.

Shiva & Parvati's Balance: Their relationship demonstrated both

individuality and unity, showing that personal growth and companionship can coexist.
Each of these sacred bonds teaches us that our own relationships can serve as a beacon of love and harmony.

How Your Marriage Can Positively Influence Others

For Your Children: The way you interact with your spouse teaches your children how relationships should function. They learn about love, respect, and partnership by observing you.
For Younger Couples: Those who are newly married or facing challenges in their relationships often look for role models. Your journey—filled with lessons and growth—can provide valuable guidance.
For Your Community: A strong and harmonious relationship contributes to a society that values love, commitment, and understanding.

Ways to Lead by Example

Show Love in Simple Ways: Small gestures like a warm smile, a heartfelt compliment, or a caring touch reinforce the presence of love.
Communicate with Respect: Even in moments of disagreement, model active listening, patience, and understanding.
Share Your Wisdom: Offer advice and support to younger couples or those who seek guidance on maintaining a happy marriage.
Teach Through Actions: Express gratitude and kindness at home so your children grow up understanding what a loving relationship looks like.
Support Your Spouse Publicly: Acknowledge your partner's efforts and stand by them in social settings, showing that love thrives in mutual respect.

Today's Action Step: Be a Model of Love and Commitment

Choose one way to demonstrate love and respect in your marriage today—whether it's a kind word, a thoughtful act, or a moment of quality time. Your example will not only strengthen your bond but also inspire those around you.

A loving marriage isn't just a personal blessing—it's a source of light for others to follow. ❤

DAY 32: STRENGTHEN YOUR BOND THROUGH SERVICE – SERVE TOGETHER

Find a way to give back as a couple.

Timeless Wisdom:
"Sevā paramo dharmaḥ."
"Service is the highest duty." – Mahabharata

Love Grows When You Serve Together

A fulfilling marriage extends beyond personal happiness—it thrives when partners work together for a greater good. Acts of kindness and service strengthen your bond, deepen your compassion, and add purpose to your relationship. By serving as a team, you cultivate shared values and experience the joy of making a difference together.

Serving others fosters gratitude, empathy, and teamwork. It shifts focus from daily routines to something bigger, reinforcing the foundation of love and mutual respect.

Lessons from Sacred Partnerships

Rama & Sita's Dedication to Their Kingdom: Despite facing exile, they remained committed to their duty, setting an example of selfless leadership.

Krishna & Rukmini's Generosity: Lord Krishna and Rukmini extended their love beyond their relationship by helping those in need, teaching that love flourishes when shared with others.

Shiva & Parvati's Balance of Love and Responsibility: Their

union was not just about devotion to each other but also about guiding and uplifting the world.
These divine examples show that when a couple joins hands in service, they nurture a deeper connection and build a legacy of love and generosity.

How Serving Together Strengthens Your Marriage

Creates Shared Purpose: Working towards a common goal fosters unity and strengthens your sense of partnership.
Inspires Gratitude: Helping others reminds you to appreciate the blessings in your own life.
Builds Compassion: Acts of kindness deepen your understanding and empathy as a couple.
Brings Joy and Fulfillment: Giving back nurtures happiness, enriching your emotional and spiritual bond.

Ways to Give Back as a Couple
Volunteer Together: Spend time at a community kitchen, animal shelter, or charity organization.
Help Someone Close to You: Support a friend, neighbor, or relative who may be struggling.
Engage in Spiritual Service: Assist at a place of worship, participate in charitable events, or contribute to religious gatherings.
Support a Social Cause: Get involved in environmental efforts, education initiatives, or fundraising for a meaningful purpose.

Mentor or Guide Others: Share your experiences and wisdom to help young couples, students, or those in need.

Today's Action Step: Serve with Love

Choose one way you and your spouse can give back today. It could be as simple as donating to a cause, helping someone in need, or planning a long-term service project together.

When you serve as a team, you don't just uplift others—you strengthen your love, build a meaningful partnership, and create a marriage rooted in purpose and kindness.

DAY 33: CELEBRATE MILESTONES – HONOR YOUR JOURNEY TOGETHER

Acknowledge and cherish your journey.

Timeless Wisdom:

"Smṛtir anantā."

"Memories last forever." – Vedic Hymn

Embracing the Special Moments in Your Relationship

Every relationship is a unique journey filled with love, learning, and shared experiences. Taking time to celebrate important milestones—whether big or small—strengthens your bond and reminds you of the journey you've traveled together.

Milestones aren't just anniversaries; they include the day you met, your first trip together, overcoming challenges, or any moment that defines your relationship. Acknowledging these moments deepens appreciation and keeps love fresh and meaningful.

Lessons from Timeless Love Stories

Rama & Sita: Despite facing separation and hardships, their reunion symbolized unwavering devotion and the joy of cherishing togetherness.

Krishna & Radha: Their love was a continuous celebration, filled with meaningful exchanges and moments of pure connection.

Shiva & Parvati: They honored their union through rituals, conversations, and mutual respect, showing that every shared moment holds significance.

These stories highlight that love isn't only about grand gestures —it's about treasuring everyday moments and recognizing the milestones that shape a relationship.

Why Celebrating Milestones Matters

Strengthens Emotional Connection: Acknowledging your journey reminds you of the love and effort invested in your relationship.
Encourages Gratitude: Reflecting on your time together fosters appreciation for one another.
Brings Joy & Excitement: Celebrating keeps your relationship lively and adds an element of surprise and warmth.
Marks Growth as a Couple: Every milestone represents progress—whether it's learning from challenges or achieving goals together.

Ways to Celebrate Milestones Together

Revisit a Special Place: Return to where you first met or recreate a cherished moment.
Create a Memory Collection: Compile photos, notes, or keepsakes that represent your journey together.
Express Your Appreciation: Write a heartfelt letter highlighting your love and shared growth.
Plan a Romantic Evening: Whether it's a dinner, a quiet night under the stars, or an activity you both love, make it meaningful.
Give a Thoughtful Surprise: A handwritten note, a small token of appreciation, or a spontaneous gesture can make a big difference.
Go on a Getaway: Plan a trip or a weekend retreat to celebrate and create new memories.

Today's Action Step: Reflect and Celebrate

Take a moment to think about a meaningful milestone in your relationship. Whether it's a significant anniversary or a simple memory, find a way to honor it—through words, actions, or a thoughtful gesture.

A relationship flourishes when you cherish the journey, not just the destination. Every shared moment is a reason to celebrate.

.

DAY 34: ESTABLISH MEANINGFUL TRADITIONS – STRENGTHEN YOUR BOND THROUGH SHARED RITUALS

Establish meaningful rituals for your family.

Timeless Wisdom:
"Samskāra hi jīvanam."
"Rituals and traditions shape life." – Manusmriti

Why Traditions Matter in a Relationship

Traditions serve as anchors in a relationship, providing a sense of stability, connection, and shared purpose. Whether simple daily gestures or grand annual celebrations, these rituals create a unique rhythm in your relationship, deepening your emotional bond and offering cherished memories.

Establishing traditions fosters continuity in marriage, making ordinary moments more meaningful. Whether it's a quiet evening ritual or a festive family tradition, these shared experiences strengthen love, trust, and togetherness over time.

Lessons from Timeless Relationships

Rama & Sita: Their commitment to dharma and shared responsibilities in all circumstances kept them united.
Krishna & Radha: Their bond was not only about divine love but also the joy found in shared traditions and moments of togetherness.
Shiva & Parvati: Their deep companionship was enriched by sacred rituals, meditation, and mutual devotion.

These legendary couples show us that traditions—both spiritual and personal—serve as a foundation for a strong, loving relationship.

How Traditions Strengthen Your Relationship

✓ **Creates Meaningful Connection** – Shared rituals give you dedicated time to nurture your bond.

✓ **Brings Stability and Comfort** – In a busy life, consistent traditions offer reassurance and security.

✓ **Builds a Legacy** – The traditions you establish today can be carried forward for generations.

✓ **Encourages Togetherness** – Simple rituals encourage mindfulness and appreciation for each other.

Ideas to Create Meaningful Traditions

Daily Rituals:

- Start each morning with a positive affirmation or prayer together.
- Share a cup of tea or a short walk every evening to reconnect.
- End the day with a moment of gratitude, expressing appreciation for each other.

Weekly Traditions:

- Dedicate one night to an uninterrupted "us time" – a movie night, a deep conversation, or a special meal.
- Cook a favorite meal together on a chosen day of the week.
- Have a Sunday ritual where you reflect on the past week and plan for the next one.

Annual and Special Traditions:

- Celebrate anniversaries in a unique way, such as writing letters to each other.
- Mark personal milestones—like the day you met—with a meaningful outing.
- Start a festival tradition, like decorating your home together or preparing a special dish.

Spiritual and Growth-Oriented Traditions:

- Meditate together or have a quiet reflection session.
- Read a book or scripture together, discussing insights from it.
- Volunteer or give back to the community as a couple.

Today's Challenge: Start a New Tradition

Think of a simple tradition that brings you both joy and start practicing it. Whether it's a morning hug, an evening gratitude practice, or a monthly adventure, small consistent acts of togetherness strengthen love over time.

Love thrives in the little moments. The traditions you build today will become the cherished memories of tomorrow.

DAY 35: EMBRACE CHANGE TOGETHER – NAVIGATE LIFE'S TRANSITIONS AS A TEAM

Support each other through life's transitions.

Wisdom for the Journey:
"Parivartanam anityam."
"Change is the only constant." – Vedic Teaching

Why Embracing Change Together Matters

Life is a continuous cycle of growth, transformation, and unexpected turns. Just as individuals evolve, so do relationships. A strong marriage is not about avoiding change but about adapting to it hand in hand. Whether it's a career shift, a family expansion, relocating to a new place, or overcoming personal struggles, facing these transitions as a team strengthens trust and deepens emotional connection.

Change can be challenging, but it also presents an opportunity for couples to strengthen their bond. The way you support each other during transitions defines the resilience of your relationship.

Lessons from Timeless Relationships

Sita & Rama: Their love remained steadfast through contrasting phases—luxury in a palace and hardship in exile. Their unwavering faith in each other is a testament to embracing change together.
Shiva & Parvati: Despite their differences—Shiva's ascetic lifestyle and Parvati's devotion to family life—they adapted and balanced their relationship, creating harmony through change.
Radha & Krishna: Their love transcended physical presence and circumstances, showing that emotional connection can

withstand life's changes when rooted in deep understanding.
These examples highlight that successful relationships aren't about avoiding difficulties but about facing them with love and unity.

How Adaptability Strengthens Your Marriage

✓ **Enhances Emotional Security** – Knowing you have each other's support builds confidence.

✓ **Encourages Mutual Growth** – Change pushes both partners to evolve in new ways.

✓ **Deepens Trust and Understanding** – Facing life's shifts together fosters stronger emotional bonding.

✓ **Reduces Stress and Conflict** – When both partners embrace change, transitions become smoother.

Ways to Support Each Other Through Change

Keep Open Communication:

- Share your feelings and concerns about upcoming changes.
- Listen without judgment and acknowledge each other's emotions.
- Find solutions together rather than facing challenges alone.

Be Each Other's Pillar:

- Offer words of encouragement when your spouse is feeling uncertain.
- Be patient as they adjust to new situations.
- Celebrate small victories along the way.

Adapt as a Team:

- Approach change with a positive mindset.
- Be flexible in your expectations and willing to make adjustments.
- See transitions as opportunities for personal and relationship growth.

Create a Shared Vision:

- Reflect on past challenges you've overcome together.
- Define goals and plans that align with your evolving life.

- Acknowledge that change is an essential part of a thriving marriage.

Today's Challenge: Support Your Spouse in an Ongoing Change

Think about a transition your spouse is currently experiencing—whether it's work-related, a personal goal, a health journey, or an emotional shift. Take an intentional step to support them, whether through encouragement, a kind gesture, or simply listening.

A marriage that embraces change together grows stronger with every new chapter.

FINAL DAYS: COMMITMENT & RENEWAL

Day 36: Be Each Other's Best Friend – Strengthen Your Bond Through Companionship

Day 37: Keep the Romance Alive – Nurture Love Beyond the Years

Day 38: Leave a Legacy of Love – Inspire Future Generations

Day 39: Renew Your Vows – Reaffirm Your Devotion

Day 40: Celebrate Your Love – Make This Journey Memorable

DAY 36: BE EACH OTHER'S BEST FRIEND – STRENGTHEN YOUR BOND THROUGH COMPANIONSHIP

Strengthen companionship.

Timeless Wisdom:

"Mitraṁ bhavantu sarvathaḥ."
"May we always remain friends." – Atharva Veda 6.64.2

Why Friendship is the Heart of a Happy Marriage

Love forms the foundation of a marriage, but true companionship is what keeps it strong. A couple that treats each other as best friends experiences a deeper level of connection —one that is built on trust, laughter, and mutual support. Friendship in marriage means feeling safe to be yourself, sharing dreams and struggles, and enjoying life's journey together.

When your spouse is your closest friend, you:

✓ Feel heard, valued, and understood.
✓ Find joy in the smallest moments together.
✓ Navigate challenges as a team.
✓ Strengthen your emotional and mental well-being.

A relationship rooted in friendship ensures that love isn't just a fleeting emotion but a lasting, supportive partnership.

Lessons from Sacred Friendships

Krishna & Arjuna: More than a divine guide, Krishna was a loyal friend who stood by Arjuna through every battle, offering wisdom and unwavering support.

Shiva & Parvati: Their bond was built on deep conversations, shared wisdom, and mutual admiration, showing that marriage flourishes when both partners uplift each other.

Rama & Lakshmana: Their companionship extended beyond brotherhood, proving that loyalty, sacrifice, and unconditional trust are the essence of true friendship.

These examples remind us that a marriage strengthened by friendship remains unshakable through all of life's phases.

Ways to Strengthen Friendship in Marriage

Have Meaningful Conversations:

- Share your thoughts, hopes, and even your silliest ideas.
- Listen with an open heart and without judgment.
- Laugh together—it's one of the best ways to stay emotionally close.

Engage in Fun Activities Together:

- Enjoy shared hobbies, whether it's cooking, dancing, or watching a favorite show.
- Try something new together—adventure fosters connection.
- Plan spontaneous outings or simple moments, like stargazing or taking a peaceful walk.

Be a Source of Unwavering Support:

- Encourage your spouse's goals and celebrate their successes.
- Stand by each other during tough times, offering reassurance and strength.
- Show up consistently—being dependable builds trust.

Respect and Appreciate Each Other's Individuality:

- Accept your differences rather than trying to change each other.
- Recognize that friendship thrives when both partners feel valued for who they truly are.
- Celebrate each other's uniqueness—it adds richness to your relationship.

Today's Challenge: Strengthen Your Bond Through a Simple Gesture

Choose an activity that brings you both happiness—play a game, share funny memories, or take a walk together. Prioritize laughter and connection, making time for each other without distractions.

A marriage built on friendship isn't just about staying together —it's about truly enjoying the journey together.

DAY 37: KEEP THE ROMANCE ALIVE – NURTURE LOVE BEYOND THE YEARS

Continue dating even after years of marriage

Timeless Wisdom:
"Anuragaha shashvatah."
"Love should be eternal." – Vedic Hymn

The Essence of Lasting Romance

Love isn't meant to fade with time; rather, it should grow deeper and richer as the years pass. While responsibilities and daily routines can sometimes take precedence, making an effort to keep romance alive ensures that your relationship remains vibrant and fulfilling.

Sustaining romance in marriage leads to:
✓ A stronger emotional and physical connection.
✓ Renewed appreciation and admiration for each other.
✓ A sense of excitement and adventure, no matter how long you've been together.
✓ A bond built on shared memories and experiences.

Love is not only about special occasions—it's about the small, everyday moments that reinforce your commitment and affection.

Lessons from Timeless Love Stories

Krishna & Radha: Their love transcended time, symbolizing devotion and the joy of simply being in each other's presence.

Rama & Sita: Their relationship endured trials, proving that true love is not just about happiness but also about unwavering support and faithfulness.

Shiva & Parvati: Their companionship reflected not just romance

but also deep respect, balance, and understanding.
These legendary bonds remind us that love is not just about feeling—it's about conscious effort, mutual care, and continuous appreciation.

Ways to Keep Romance Thriving

Prioritize Time Together:

- Schedule regular date nights or quiet moments just for the two of you.
- Try new activities together, whether it's a dinner, a nature walk, or a shared hobby.
- Revisit special places that hold sentimental value in your relationship.

Express Affection Daily:

- Say "I love you" with meaning, not just out of routine.
- Leave thoughtful notes or send a heartfelt message during the day.
- Offer small acts of love—like making their favorite meal or simply holding hands.

Create Thoughtful Surprises:

- Surprise your spouse with an unexpected gesture, such as breakfast in bed or a handwritten love letter.
- Give them a small but meaningful gift that shows you know what they cherish.
- Plan a spontaneous outing or celebration, just to remind them how much they mean to you.

Strengthen Emotional and Physical Intimacy:

- Physical closeness—like a gentle touch, warm hug, or playful gestures—helps maintain the connection.
- Engage in deep, meaningful conversations about dreams, aspirations, and personal growth.
- Keep the excitement alive with lighthearted flirting and playful moments.

Today's Challenge: Add a Spark of Romance

Do something romantic for your spouse today—whether it's a kind word, a small surprise, or quality time together.

Love isn't just about growing old together; it's about growing closer with each passing day.

DAY 38: LEAVE A LEGACY OF LOVE – INSPIRE FUTURE GENERATIONS

Set an example for future generations.

Timeless Wisdom:

"Vasudhaiva Kutumbakam."

"The entire world is one family." – Maha Upanishad 6.72

Love That Lasts Beyond a Lifetime

A strong and loving relationship is not just for the present —it sets an example for the future. The way you nurture your bond today influences the lives of your children, grandchildren, and even your wider community. By showing respect, patience, and devotion in your marriage, you create a blueprint for the next generation to build meaningful relationships.

A lasting partnership teaches:

✓ The importance of trust, understanding, and kindness.
✓ The strength of staying committed through life's challenges.
✓ The beauty of sharing dreams, values, and a common purpose.
✓ The power of small acts of love and appreciation in daily life.

When love is expressed consistently and sincerely, it leaves an imprint that extends far beyond a single lifetime.

Lessons from Timeless Bonds

Shiva & Parvati: Their relationship embodies balance and devotion, inspiring couples to cultivate harmony and mutual respect.

Krishna & Radha: Their love is a symbol of deep spiritual connection, reminding us that true companionship goes beyond physical presence.

Rama & Sita: Their journey highlights loyalty, sacrifice, and trust, offering lessons on navigating both joys and hardships together.

Just as these relationships have inspired generations, your love story can leave a lasting impression on those who look up to you.

Ways to Create a Legacy of Love

Be a Living Example of Love:

- Express affection and appreciation through words and actions.
- Demonstrate patience and support during difficult times.
- Show that love is not just about romance but about standing by each other in all aspects of life.

Pass Down Wisdom and Stories:

- Share meaningful experiences from your journey as a couple.
- Teach younger family members the values that strengthen a relationship, such as communication, respect, and compromise.
- Encourage open discussions about the importance of love, commitment, and emotional connection.

Establish Meaningful Family Traditions:

- Celebrate special occasions that honor your journey together.
- Create rituals that reinforce connection, like expressing gratitude daily or reminiscing over cherished memories.
- Encourage future generations to prioritize love and partnership in their own lives.

Extend Love Beyond Your Home:

- Treat friends, neighbors, and acquaintances with warmth and kindness.
- Support community initiatives as a couple, reinforcing the importance of love through service.
- Offer guidance to young couples by sharing valuable relationship insights.

Today's Challenge: Share Your Love Story

Reflect on the key moments that have strengthened your relationship. Pass down a piece of wisdom or a heartfelt story to someone younger, offering them inspiration for their own journey.

A love that is nurtured with care doesn't just stay between two people—it becomes a guiding light for generations to come.

DAY 39: RENEW YOUR VOWS – REAFFIRM YOUR DEVOTION

Reaffirm your commitment.

Timeless Wisdom:

"Saha dharmam pravartaya."

"Let us walk the path of righteousness together." – Rig Veda 10.85.42

Love is a Choice We Make Every Day

Marriage is more than a single promise made on the wedding day—it is a lifelong commitment that deepens with time. Just as seasons change, relationships evolve, and reaffirming your commitment reminds both partners of the journey you have taken together.

Renewing your vows is an opportunity to:

✓ Reflect on the memories, challenges, and victories you've shared.

✓ Acknowledge the growth and depth your relationship has gained.

✓ Strengthen your emotional connection through conscious commitment.

✓ Celebrate your bond, reminding each other why you chose this path together.

It doesn't require an extravagant ceremony—sometimes, a simple heartfelt conversation is enough to reinforce the love and devotion you share.

Lessons from Enduring Love Stories

Rama & Sita: Even through trials and separation, their faith in each other remained unwavering, teaching the value of perseverance in love.

Shiva & Parvati: Their deep understanding and mutual respect show that love thrives when both partners honor each other's strengths and differences.

Krishna & Rukmini: Their relationship exemplifies devotion and companionship, reminding us that love is nurtured through care and shared dreams.

These stories teach us that love is not just about staying together but about continuously choosing each other through every phase of life.

Ways to Reaffirm Your Devotion

Have an Honest Conversation:

- Set aside time to talk about your journey together.
- Share what you appreciate about each other and how your love has grown.
- Express gratitude for the challenges you've faced and overcome as a team.

Make a Personal Promise:

- Verbally express your commitment to one another in a meaningful moment.
- Reflect on the vows you once made and reaffirm them in your own words.
- Acknowledge the ways you will continue to support, cherish, and uplift each other.

Create a Symbolic Tradition:

- Light a candle or diya together to represent your ever-growing love.
- Revisit a place that holds special memories, like where you first met or got married.
- Write each other a heartfelt letter about your journey and future dreams.

Celebrate with Loved Ones:

- Gather family or close friends for a small ceremony or intimate celebration.
- Share your love story and inspire others by demonstrating commitment in action.
- If meaningful, partake in a traditional ritual together, such as walking hand in hand in a sacred space.

Today's Challenge: Express Your Commitment in a Special Way

Take a moment today to look into your spouse's eyes and say, *"I choose you, today and always."* Whether through words, actions, or a small but meaningful gesture, remind them that your love remains strong and unwavering.

True love isn't just about saying 'I do' once—it's about reaffirming it every single day in the little moments that matter.

DAY 40: CELEBRATE YOUR LOVE – MAKE THIS JOURNEY MEMORABLE

Recommit your love and tell them why you would choose them each time.

Timeless Wisdom:

"Ananda mayo bhyasat."

"Joy is our true nature." – Taittiriya Upanishad 2.7

Love is a Gift to Be Cherished

A strong relationship is not just about overcoming challenges together but also about celebrating the moments that make your journey special. In the midst of responsibilities, it's easy to overlook the beauty of your bond. Taking time to appreciate each other reinforces the love and commitment that hold your relationship together.

Celebrating love doesn't require a grand gesture—it's about recognizing and valuing your partnership in meaningful ways. Whether through small acts of kindness, heartfelt conversations, or shared traditions, every effort strengthens the connection between you and your spouse.

Lessons from Timeless Love Stories

Krishna & Radha: Their bond was full of joy and devotion, showing us that love flourishes when nurtured with playfulness and care.

Rama & Sita: Despite facing immense hardships, they found strength in each other, reminding us that true love is about unwavering support.

Shiva & Parvati: Their deep connection teaches the importance of mutual respect and cherishing every moment together.

These legendary couples inspire us to celebrate our own relationships, making them stronger through gratitude and appreciation.

Ways to Celebrate Your Love

Create a Special Moment Together

- Plan a quiet evening with a home-cooked meal or a favorite activity.
- Revisit a meaningful place, such as where you first met or had your first date.
- Take a peaceful walk together, reminiscing about your journey so far.

Reflect on Your Relationship

- Look through old pictures and recall happy memories.
- Share what you admire about each other and express appreciation for your journey together.
- Write a heartfelt note expressing gratitude and love for your partner.

Honor Your Love in a Spiritual Way

- Offer prayers together, seeking blessings for your continued happiness.
- Light a diya or candle as a symbol of your enduring love.
- Meditate together or engage in a spiritual practice that brings you both peace.

Establish a New Tradition

- Create a special ritual, like setting aside a day each month for a date night.
- Keep a journal of meaningful moments and milestones in your relationship.
- Start a habit of sharing one thing you appreciate about each other every day.

Today's Challenge: Celebrate Your Love with a Thoughtful Gesture

As this 40-day journey comes to an end, take a moment to honor the love you've cultivated. Whether through a quiet evening together, a heartfelt conversation, or a symbolic act, find a way to express appreciation for your relationship.

True love isn't just about lasting through the years—it's about making every moment meaningful.